Steve Wright started his professional life as a marine insurance broker. After a few stops and starts, he found himself in newspaper journalism, from which he moved into local commercial radio in the early 80s. He went on to host the popular talk and music programmes *Steve Wright in the Afternoon* and *Steve Wright in the Morning* for BBC Radio 1. He left Radio 1 in 1995 to host the popular BBC TV programme, *The People Show*, and is looking forward to returning soon to daily radio.

STEVE WRIGHT'S

BOOK OF THE

AMAZING BUT TRUE

Trivia For the Connoisseur

POCKET
BOOKS

LONDON · SYDNEY · NEW YORK · TOKYO · SINGAPORE · TORONTO

First published in Great Britain by Pocket Books, 1995
An imprint of Simon & Schuster Ltd

Simon & Schuster Ltd
West Garden Place
Kendal Street
London W2 2AQ

Simon & Schuster of Australia Pty Ltd
Sydney

A CIP catalogue record for this book is available from the
British Library

ISBN 0-671-85482-8

Typeset in Meridien & Gill Sans 10/13pt by
Palimpsest Book Production Limited, Polmont, Stirlingshire
Printed and bound in Great Britain by
HarperCollins Manufacturing, Glasgow

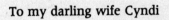
To my darling wife Cyndi

To the millions who know Steve Wright from his popular Radio and TV shows, he seems a rather tame family man. But beneath the moustache and glasses lurks a guy whose fascination with the bizarre and unusual borders on the unhealthy . . . This book is testament to that fascination. After reading it you'll know for certain YOU are normal and HE IS TWISTED.

CONTENTS

1
ALL TIME LOSERS

Welcome to our all time losers section. Some are part-time losers, some are instant losers and some are outright saddos.

Abel Ruiz of Madrid decided to kill himself in 1978 after being thwarted in love. He threw himself under the Gerona to Madrid express but suffered only minor injuries. He was released from hospital and then jumped under a passing lorry but once again his injuries were minor. On his return to hospital he was seen by a priest who managed to talk him out of his suicidal state and persuaded him to try to relaunch his life with a new girlfriend. On leaving hospital with new resolve he was accidentally hit by a runaway horse and suffered serious injuries.

Public official Keith Osbourne was one of the UK's leading beer bottle label collectors and a regular visitor to the Public Record Office where he admired the government archive of said labels. Overcome with envy he smuggled the rarest bottles to the nearest lavatory where he attempted to soak the labels off in a cistern. Unbeknown to him his actions were being recorded by a security camera and Osbourne found himself in court. He was sentenced to eighteen months in jail. His wife exploded after the case: 'It's ridiculous, if he had killed somebody he'd have got twenty-eight days and a holiday to go with it.'

Friendless Chilean spinster Isabella Vasquez sought the answer to a barren sex life by coating herself in dog food and allowing her pet poodle to lick it off her naked body. Unknown to her, members of her family had arranged a surprise party to cheer her up and were waiting outside the house to enter. As they burst in the sight that met their eyes caused her father to collapse and the rest of the family to recoil in horror. Vasquez was later advised to seek psychiatric counselling.

F. W. Murnau was one of Germany's leading film directors in the 1920s and arrived to work in Hollywood on the strength of such horror classics as *Nosferatu*. En route to New York from Hollywood in 1931 for the premiere of his film *Tabu* he consulted an astrologer on the best way to travel. He was told to take a boat from San Francisco through the Panama Canal. In the car on the way to the port he decided to administer a blow job to his 14-year-old Filipino houseboy who was at the wheel. The boy lost control of the car, killing Murnau in the resultant crash.

Rob Pilatus and Fabrice Morvan achieved worldwide fame as Milli Vanilli with hits such as 'Blame It on the Rain', 'Girl I'm Gonna Miss You' and 'Baby Don't Forget My Number'. They won America's prestigious Grammy award as best new artists in 1989. However, rumours circulated throughout the record industry that they did not sing on their records. Their producer Frank Farian finally bowed to pressure and admitted the voices on the records were that of a middle-aged former US soldier, Brad Howell, and his partner John Davis. Farian claimed Pilatus and Morvan were only interested in

Eight out of ten relatives said their dogs preferred her.

partying down all night and sleeping the next day. Their Grammy was withdrawn and Pilatus later failed in a suicide attempt when he dangled from the railings of the top floor of LA's Mondrian hotel. He was rescued by the fire brigade after a tip-off from the *LA Times* who he had conveniently rung advising of his intentions.

US child star Bobby Driscoll was a major actor by the age of six and an Oscar winner at the age of eleven. He became Walt Disney's first contracted human 'flesh and blood' actor and is remembered for his roles in *Song of the South* and *Treasure Island*. He won special acclaim for his role in *The Window*, a 1949 drama set in New York's Lower East Side. Nineteen years later a body was found in the same New York location in a seedy tenement surrounded by religious objects. Nearly two years later Driscoll's father on his deathbed expressed a last wish to see his son and the Disney company set out to track him down. They discovered Driscoll was the man found in the tenement having turned to a life of drugs and crime when his acting career faltered. *Song of the South* was re-released in 1972 and became a major money spinner for Disney once more.

A Mexican starlet Lupe Velez planned the perfect suicide in 1944. The former wife of Tarzan star Johnny Weismuller took seventy-five seconal tablets in her palatial bedroom surrounded by flowers and candles. She lay on a satin-covered bed with her hands joined in prayer imagining the newspaper headlines the next day of the death of 'Sleeping Beauty'. This scene was diminished somewhat the next morning when her maid arrived to find a trail of vomit to the bathroom.

Velez was found drowned, her head jammed in the toilet bowl.

A butcher in Germany was killed when he was about to slaughter a pig with a shotgun. The pig raised its trotter in fear and set off the trigger, killing the man instantly.

Angelo Ricci was an 80s high flyer with a BMW and salary to match. But when the Thatcher era ended a London court heard how the former whiz kid was reduced to travelling on the London tube. He had been arrested for stealing a woman's purse and his defence claimed this was because of his unfamiliarity with public transport. His solicitor explained that the sight of money had sickened him and he had tried to make a run for it before being apprehended by the transport police. Angelo was found guilty and sentenced to jail.

Russia's version of the Concorde nicknamed Concordski crashed on its very first public appearance. A second one was built but was only ever used to transport mail.

Louis Le Prince should have been revered as the inventor of motion pictures. He demonstrated the movie-making process at the Paris Opera in 1890 and was all set on the road to riches and fame. He disappeared on a train journey later that year and was never seen again. He was declared dead seven years later although his body was never found. His innovative techniques were later exploited by Thomas Edison who is now credited with his ideas.

In 1787 Jabez Spicer was shot dead by two bullets at the Federal Arsenal, Springfield, Mass. He was wearing a coat owned by his brother Daniel who had been shot dead by two bullets three years before. The bullets passed through the same two holes.

Arthur Sharland, a retired heating engineer from Shepherd's Bush, was found dead in 1989 in his flat with two crocodile clips attached to his body running to the mains. At the post mortem neighbours told the coroner he regularly plugged himself into the mains as it 'turned him on'.

Robert Puelo stole a hot dog from a fast food store in St Louis, Missouri and he attempted to swallow it whole when apprehended by the shop owner. He collapsed on the pavement and though medics frantically tried to remove the six-inch frankfurter lodged in his throat, Puelo choked to death.

Griffith Morgan, an eighteenth-century Welsh sportsman, ran twelve miles in fifty-three minutes and was given a hundred gold sovereigns as a prize. Shortly after the race he collapsed and died after receiving a friendly slap on the back.

During World War I French intelligence captured German spy Peter Karpin, sent fake intelligence reports in his name and recouped all the money the spy was paid by his masters. The French used the funds to buy a new car for their department. Peter Karpin was accidentally run over in 1919 at the war's end by the same car.

In 1948 sculptor Korczak Ziolkowski began work on a giant mountainside sculpture of red Indian chief Crazy Horse just sixteen miles from the famous Mount Rushmore monument depicting four former US presidents. He died in 1982 having removed seven million tons of rock from the mountain face, but his task still was unfinished. His wife and ten children are still now employed trying to finish the sculpture which will be 563 feet high and 641 feet long.

In March 1962 Bill Giles died in Broadmoor Prison aged eighty-seven. He had been incarcerated there in 1886 at the age of eleven. A Broadmoor spokesman said, 'He got on well with everyone. He was never any trouble and knew the daily routine so well that he often corrected new nurses if they did not keep strictly to the timetable.' He spent his first five years in the women's wards as a child and then was allowed to enter the men's wards to live with murderers and rapists. Bill's crime: he had set fire to a haystack.

In 1883 Texan Henry Ziegland jilted his sweetheart and her irate brother pursued him with a shotgun but missed him, hitting a tree instead and inflicting only minor injuries on the love cheat. The distraught brother committed suicide thinking he had killed Ziegland whom he had only intended to frighten. In 1913 Ziegland demolished the tree using dynamite and was instantly killed when the bullet ricocheted out wounding him mortally during the explosion.

Here comes a saddo then: astrologer Girolamo Cardano predicted his death on 21 September 1576. When he felt fine for most of the day he decided to make his prediction come true by commiting suicide.

On 30 May 1867 Princess Maria Del Pozzo Della Cisterna and Amadeo the Duke D'Aosta, the son of the King of Italy, got married. On that day the Princess' wardrobe mistress hung herself, the palace gatekeeper cut his throat and the colonel leading the procession collapsed with sunstroke. The local station master was crushed to death under a train, the King's aide was killed after a fall from his horse and the best man shot himself. The couple did not live happily ever after.

Hungarian game hunter Endre Bascany was shot dead by other hunters because his impersonation of a stag's mating call was so accurate.

Tramps Billy O'Rourke and Pat Burke died shortly after receiving their first baths in twenty years in St Louis, Missouri in 1903.

World snail-eating champion Marc Quinquadon set out to beat his record of consuming 144 snails in 11 minutes 30 seconds in 1979. Unfortunately he collapsed and died at snail number 72 in the third minute.

Colonel Pierrepoint was responsible for erecting the first traffic island in Piccadilly. Stepping back to admire his handiwork he was run over and killed by a hansom cab.

Kokichi Tsuburaya of Japan won bronze for Japan at the 1964

Olympics and then promptly committed suicide because he felt he had let down his country.

In the war of 1812 US General William H. Winder was unsurpassed as one of the worst military commanders in history. At the Battle of Stony Creek he lost despite a four-to-one troop superiority over the British. The clever Brits captured him but allowed him to return to his own side in the hope he could create even greater military disasters. He didn't fail them. He allowed Washington to be captured and razed to the ground.

A man who held up a bank in Portland, Oregon, in 1969 wrote all his messages to the cashier whilst in the bank. He began with, 'This is a hold up and I've got a gun,' following up with, 'Put all your money in a paper bag.' The cashier entered into the spirit of the robbery by writing, 'I don't have a paper bag.' The inept robber took fright at this and ran off.

A Kansas City jewel thief repeatedly robbed a jewellery store by smashing the front window with a brick. The desperate owner installed an unbreakable plastic window and police were called to the scene when passers-by reported an unconscious man outside lying next to a brick which had rebounded and knocked him out cold.

2
BETS

Horse owner and politician Horatio Bottomley placed what he thought was the perfect bet in a horse race at Blankenberghe, Belgium. He owned the entire field of six horses and employed six English jockeys, advising them in which order he wanted them to finish. Halfway through the race a thick coastal fog descended on the course and the race was declared null and void. Bottomley lost a fortune with his stake money.

In 1984 Mike Wittkowski won a record $40 million dollars in the Illinois State Lottery, his ticket cost just $35.

Delores Adams won almost $1 million dollars on a fruit machine at the Reno Hotel, Nevada, in 1992.

Trevor Thomas, a hospital gardener, has staked £10 at 5–1 that he will outlive jockey Lester Piggott. Both men are fifty-eight. Mr Thomas owns up to a bad back, is a lager drinker and enjoys fish and chips while Piggott enjoys a healthy outdoor life. Mr Thomas claims, however, there's nothing Lester Piggott wouldn't do to spite a bookie.

Scotsman James Orr has placed a £25 bet at 10,000–1 that his eight-year-old footballing son will score a goal for England in the World Cup final of 2006.

Fruitful winnings – Dolores Adams hits the jackpot.

Charles Wells was not a professional gambler but he found fame, being immortalised in the song 'The Man Who Broke the Bank at Monte Carlo'. He won the 'bank' of 100,000 francs three times in 1891. Twice he put even money on black and red, winning nearly early time. He then bet on number five at 35–1 and won. He left his original bet and added his winnings and won again. He did that five times and each time the number five came up.

John Moores and two partners began their pools company Littlewoods in the 1920s whilst still employed by the Commercial Cable Company. The company name was taken from one of the partners whose family name it was. Their first effort attracted just thirty-five paying customers bringing in £4.17s.6d. and a first dividend of £2.12s.0.d.

Anthony S. Clancy of Dublin, Ireland, was born on the seventh day of the week, on the seventh day of the month in the seventh year of this century. He was the seventh child of a seventh child and had seven brothers. On his twenty-seventh birthday whilst attending a horse race he bet on horse number seven called Seventh Heaven to win the seventh race on the card at 7–1. The race was a seven-stone handicap. His seven-shilling bet gave him no return as his horse came in seventh.

If it's possible to have very good and very bad luck on the same day this has to be the shining example. When Englishman Robert Fallon was shot dead playing cards in 1858 at the Bella Union Saloon in San Francisco after being accused of cheating, a passer-by was asked to take his place at the table. He promptly won $2,200 dollars. Since money won by cheating was considered unlucky the police attempted to track down Fallon's next of kin to repay him $600 that he had won. They discovered that the stranger who had taken his place at the table was his son who had not seen his father for seven years.

If a croupier points to his ear in a casino at the gaming table you know someone is on a winning streak. It's a signal for help from other casino staff.

In 1956 Californian paint manufacturer Jack Slimmer predicted the number of votes to be cast for General Dwight D. Eisenhower in the US election. He sealed them in a bank vault along with a cheque for $5,000 payable to charity if he was wrong and had everything verified by a Los Angeles charity commissioner. He predicted 1,218,462 votes in Los Angeles County, 2,875,637 votes in California and 33,974,241 in the rest of the country. When the results were declared his numbers were 100 per cent accurate. Had he made a wager he would no doubt have won a fortune but he was so happy he gave the money to charity anyway.

In 1907 US millionaire John Pierpoint Morgan bet Lord Lonsdale $100,000 that a man could walk around the world without anyone seeing his face. Morgan employed playboy Harry Bensley to make the attempt wearing an iron mask. Bizarre rules were introduced to make his task even harder. He was only allowed to set out with £1 in his pocket, he had to push a pram and was only allowed a change of underwear. He had to find a wife without revealing his identity or face and was only allowed to sell postcards to earn money. A paid escort would accompany him to ensure the rules were adhered to. Setting off from Trafalgar Square he managed to sell a postcard to King Edward VII at Newmarket races. The king asked for his autograph but the request was rejected by Bensley's aide who said it would reveal his identity. He was arrested in Bexleyheath for selling postcards without a Street Trader's licence and was fined 2/6 by a magistrate for refusing to remove his mask in court. By August 1914 he had reached Genoa in Italy with only six countries left to travel to and 200 offers of marriage. He decided to give up, however, to serve his country in the First World War and the bet was called off. He was awarded £4,000 in consolation by Morgan and Lonsdale which he promptly gave to charity. Bensley lost most of his investments in Russia after the revolution and died in a Brighton bedsit in 1956.

3
BORING

Heston service station on the M4 is more than the location of Julie's Pantry. The complex is built on the site of Heston aerodrome where on 30 September 1938 Prime Minister Neville Chamberlain returned from his meeting with Herr Hitler waving a piece of white paper and declaring, 'I believe it is peace in our time.'

Lost for opening conversational gambits at dinner parties where you know no one? The current edition of Debrett's *Etiquette and Modern Manners* offers the following ice breakers. '"What a cold December we are having. If you weren't in England where would you like to be at this time of the year?" "If you were the Queen what opera/ballet/play would you choose to have performed for your gala?" "Are you a Wimbledon fan? Have you been watching it?" (Adjust sports seasonally if you are sufficiently knowledgeable).'

The *Bookseller* magazine ran a competition recently to find the book with the oddest title of the year. Competition rules stipulated that the work had to be of serious intent and non-fiction. The winner was C. C. Stanley's *Highlights in the History of Concrete*. Runners up included *The Illustrated History of Metal Lunchboxes*, *The Development of Brain and Behaviour in the Chicken* and *Thermal Movements in the Upper Floor of a Multi-Storey Car Park*. Special mention was also given to

Cesspools – A Do-It-Yourself Guide, and *Butchering Livestock At Home*.

With the reunification of Germany the most notorious motorway service station in the world is being handed back to the German people. Adolf Hitler regularly stopped on the shores of Chiemsee on the Munich/Salzburg autobahn and loved the area so much he had his own service station built. Hitler and friends were served hamburgers and steaks by Bavarian girls in national costume in a farmhouse-style complex decorated with rural scenes and marble sculptures which paid homage to the Aryan form. A discreet sign on the wall bears the legend 'Designed By Adolf Hitler'. US forces were based there after the war but a remodelled version will open soon for all autobahn users.

Ken Dodd, Elaine Paige, Malcolm McDowell, Max Wall and Larry Grayson have all appeared in the TV soap *Crossroads*.

A fungal infection known as *brytococcus neoformans* can fester inside bagpipes and cause disease in the player's lungs.

The 85-hour-long film *The Cure For Insomnia* received its world premiere in Chicago in 1987. It consisted of poet L. D. Groban reading his 4,080 page poem also titled 'The Cure For Insomnia' interspersed with scenes from porno films and footage of rock band J. T. 4 and Cosmic Lightning. A shorter 80-hour version was later released, minus the sex scenes.

In 1974 the University of Leeds presented a Golden Pillow

Award to the most boring lecturer on the campus. The clear winner was Dr Ashley Clark who in a special competitive lecture expounded on 'mechanical formalism of emulsion in an infinite viscous medium'. He told his audience, 'I was going to call it – "the classic hydraulic formalism of emulsion in an infinite viscous medium" but I didn't want to excite you all. This of course only applies in an infinite viscous medium so in practice it doesn't work.'

The Eskimo language has twenty different words for snow.

The legendary Noele Gordon's mother Jockey was the very first person to be seen on screen when *Crossroads* went on air in 1964. In line with its famous budgetary restraint ATV neglected to hire an extra for the opening scene so Jockey stepped out of the audience to help out.

A Consumers Association report in 1987 claimed over 2,500 people a year need medical help for injuries caused by deckchairs.

Many flute players suffer from 'flautist's chin', a medical complaint caused by dribbling which leads to a fungal infection on the lower face.

Elephants are not allowed to be led through the approach tunnel to London Airport.

Dogs in London drop four tons of excrement and 3,000 pints of urine on to the streets every day. Metallurgists have major problems preventing corrosion of London's lamp-posts caused by the deposits of doggies.

Glass blowers in Bristol used to regularly eat snails to improve their blowing power.

A man working in a mild climate loses up to five pints of sweat a day, but a miner working underground can lose thirteen pints on a single shift.

The paper 'Personality Functions of Graphic Constrictedness and Expansiveness' by Wallach and Gahm published in 1960 came to the conclusion that extroverts draw more intricate doodles than introverts.

The 134th meeting of the American Association for the Advancement of Science revealed that after considerable research it had been discovered if you burst a paper bag next to a Jersey cow the frightened animal would give a milk flow for almost thirty minutes.

Barristers in the UK still dress in all-black garb in court because they are still officially in mourning for Mary, wife of William III, who died in 1694.

The word 'bumph' in relation to piles of paperwork originates from World War II slang for toilet paper, i.e. bum fodder.

It is illegal to fish off Bournemouth Pier with two rods at the same time.

Swedish actors believe that being kicked up the backside before a performance brings good luck.

Chile has no public lavatories.

One of the earliest excursions organised on Britain's railway system was to see a public hanging at Bodmin jail.

It is still an offence under English law to demolish a hovel in a 'riotous manner'.

The first man to be convicted of a crime in the UK by fingerprint evidence was Harry Jackson in 1902. He stole some billiard balls.

In 1986 Hendy Farquhar-Smith scored twenty-one points in the specialist round of *Mastermind*. His subject was the life of swimmer David Wilkie.

Intercity serves 1.2 million pots of jam, 37 tons of bacon, 37 tons of sausages and over one million eggs every year. It also has more onboard chefs than any other railway in the world.

Dave Lockwood of the US holds the record as the longest-reigning tiddlywink champion in the world. He became the top winker in August 1978 and held the title until October 1982.

The following subjects have all been submitted to *Mastermind* for the specialist round: routes to anywhere in mainland Britain from Letchworth; cremation law and practice in Britain; the banana industry; orthopaedic bone cement in total hip replacement; farm wagons and carts of England and Wales.

I'm a regular borrower at my local library and you'll most likely find me in the large print section but I'd have trouble reading past the first page of some of these books which have all been published in the last fifty years.

Timber Framed Buildings In Watford
Jaws and Teeth of Ancient Hawaiians
Truncheons – Their Romance and Reality
A Toddler's Guide to the Rubber Industry
Bead Making in Scandinavia in the Early Middle Ages
The Music of the Mongols
Penis Sheaths and Their Distribution In Africa
Manhole Covers of Los Angeles
The Book of Practical Candle Magic
A Practical Guide for Inspectors of Nuisances
Some Account of the Beard and the Moustachio
Who's Who In Cocker Spaniels
The Benefit of Farting Explained
Constipation and Our Civilisation
Frog Raising For Pleasure and Profit
Enjoy Your Chameleon
Sex Instruction For Irish Farmers
Working With British Rail
The Wit of Prince Philip
Twenty Most Asked Questions About the Amish and
    Mennonites
A Handbook On Hanging
Be Bold With Bananas
Who's Who In Australian Embroidery
Keeping Your Tools Tiptop
And There I Stood With My Piccolo In My Hand
Explorations at Sodom
Queer Doings in the Navy

The Institute of Social Research at the University of Michigan published a list of the most boring jobs in the US based on interviews with over 2,000 employees. The winner was factory production plant assembler followed by relief worker on an assembly line and fork lift truck driver.

4
CULTS AND RELIGIONS

Old big-nose Barry Manilow subscribes to the teachings of Lazaris, a disembodied spirit who is summoned up by Jack Purser, a medium from Palm Beach, Florida.

Seventy-eight people died in New Delhi, India, after the bus they were travelling in fell into a river. Nearly all could have been saved but because they were from different castes they refused to share the single rescue rope offered.

Mormon leader Brigham Young labelled fly front trousers 'Fornication Pants'.

The Babylonian cult of Ishtar required every woman to sleep with a stranger at least once in her life at the local temple. This was felt to reflect the dual nature of womankind as mother and prostitute.

Many religions in sixth-century Europe believed the souls of the dead were transported to England by Breton fisherman.

Roman emperor Commodus demanded that his subjects worshipped him as Herakles Secundus. One of his main pastimes was organising gladiatorial contests between crippled men or stepping into the arena himself to take on unarmed opponents.

During the Spanish Inquisition all torture instruments were regularly dowsed with holy water.

Before the fifteenth century in England it was a crime punishable by death to produce a bible in any other language but Latin.

In 1982, thirty-five-year-old father of eight Roger Cox cut off his penis and threw it into the fire at his home in Denbigh, Wales as his wife joined him in prayer. He did it to devote himself 100 per cent to a life of prayer.

The head of the Californian Breatharian Institute, Wiley Brooks, lost all his followers after he was spotted by some of his disciples eating a chicken pie in a hotel restaurant. He had taught his cult members that he had not eaten for nineteen years and lived entirely on fresh air.

When Britain ruled India the authorities acted quickly to stamp out the cult of the 'Thuggee' or 'Thug' whose devotees believed that by murdering strangers they appeased the gods. There are reports, however, that the cult has been revived in some areas as recently in the 1980s. It is estimated that since the sixteenth century the Thuggees have claimed over two million victims. Some reformed Thuggees in the nineteenth century became weavers and presented a rug to Queen Victoria which is still kept at Windsor Castle.

The tomb of Chinese emperor Wen Di was discovered in 1983 and contained the bodies of six of his servants who

Roger Cox(less).

had been killed to serve him in the afterlife. The bodies of four of his concubines were also found nearby.

The Native American Church was founded in 1918 by Comanche war leader Quanah Parker. Today over half of all Native Americans belong to the religion which mixes Christian belief with the practise of chewing the peyote cactus, a hallucinatory drug.

The most murderous religion in history was that of the Aztecs who demanded on average 20,000 victims a year. Priests warned followers that their chief deity the Sun would disappear if not appeased by human sacrifice. Crying children were executed so that their tears would make the rain god water crops whilst virgins were decapitated and skinned to provide robes for priests. In 1487 eight teams of priests worked overtime arranging the ritual slaughter of 20,000 prisoners from three different tribes.

Two people were killed in Phnom Penh, Cambodia in 1972 when troops opened fire at the moon. They were trying to prevent an eclipse caused they thought by the mythical frog Reahon. According to ancient Cambodian legend the giant frog is attempting to eat the moon and must be stopped at all costs.

The American branch of the Druid religion was created in 1963 as a joke by US teenagers at school as a rebellion against formal church services. It now has many committed members.

In 1975 the Festival of Light, the crusading group

campaigning to clean up Britain, announced plans to open a hostel in London for pornography fans and sexual deviants. Volunteers would submit to a compulsory course of spiritual activities and handicrafts.

The first female security woman employed by the Vatican was a nun. Sister Fiorella (Little Flower) taken on to politely refuse admittance to women wearing mini-skirts, see-through blouses and low-cut sweaters. Church authorities reasoned no one would take issue with a kindly nun but the good Sister retired in 1971 with a nervous breakdown.

In Tel Aviv in 1957 Rabbi Ovadia Barati was imprisoned for eighteen months for obtaining money by false pretences. A Brazilian estate agent, Mr Meoded, had paid him £2,000 on the promise that the rabbi could contact Archangels Gabriel, Raphael and Michael to anoint him as the new messiah, King of Israel. The rabbi told him the angels wanted the money as a test of faith and he was given a selection of packages only to be opened when a sign was given. The inquisitive Mr Meoded opened one parcel out of curiosity only to find a selection of rocks and roof tiles. Police convicted Barati after proving letters signed 'God Almighty' had been written with his typewriter. Receipted payments marked c/o Rabbi Barati clinched the case.

In 1872 the Reverend George Philip of Saltcoats, Ayrshire, jokingly told his Sunday School class that he would give any of them £1 if they could write out the entire Old Testament within one year. Thinking no more about it he was amazed when one of his pupils, ten-year-old Robert Millar, presented him with 2,000 quarto sheets of paper of the Old Testament, the labour of six solid months. When the news spread of the boy's achievement people were appalled at the Reverend's alleged meanness. The lad was later awarded £20 after a whip round by the congregation.

Emperor Mejelik II of Ethiopia tried to preserve his health by regularly consuming chapters of the Bible.

An erotic highlight of Japan's red light districts is a form of striptease called 'Tokudashi'. The audience are given torches and binoculars to get a closer look at the stripper's body. The whole act is based on a Shinto legend that sun goddess Amaterasu once denied light to the world but a strip by fellow goddess Ama-No-Azume made other gods applaud so loudly Amaterasu came out to see the show and light was restored.

In 1992 British druids elected their first female leader in 200 years. Dwina Murphy-Gibb is the wife of Bee Gee Robin.

Creighton Miller of Altadena, California, amputated his own left foot after stepping on an insect. He believed he had sinned against God and needed to redeem himself. Naturally he hopped home.

King George I granted a patent to inventor James Puckle to produce a machine gun which could be adjusted to fire round bullets at Christians and square bullets at Turks.

The village of Staphorst in the Netherlands is one of the

last regions of the country where the Reformed Association Church holds sway. Under their strict laws no girl can be married until she is pregnant, no one is permitted to have sex on Sundays and cocks and hens are also kept apart on that day.

Under strict religious rules in India any man found guilty of seducing the wife of his guru would be made to sit on a heated iron plate and then chop off his own penis.

5

ENTERTAINMENT

Pope John Paul II wrote a play, *The Jeweller's Shop*, when he was auxiliary bishop of Krakow, Poland. A series of monologues on marriage, it was performed on the London stage in 1982.

Hammer Films were renowned from the 1950s onwards as masters of the horror film with a string of successes like *Dracula*, *Frankenstein Must Be Destroyed* and *The Hound of the Baskervilles*. However, their biggest commercial success was in 1971 with the big-screen version of top ITV comedy *On the Buses*, the biggest grossing release in the UK that year, and it certainly grossed me out.

Film star Humphrey Bogart is buried with a silver whistle bearing the legend 'If you need anything just whistle', a constant reminder of the first film he made with his wife Lauren Bacall, *To Have and Have Not*.

If you're in your late thirties like me (not!) you'll know of puppet favourite Andy Pandy who made his/her debut on BBC on 11 July 1950 and was repeated continually through almost twenty years using the same original twenty-six shows.

Where are they now? Four actresses who have won an

Oscar in the last twenty-five years. Lee Grant, Beatrice Straight, Maureen Stapleton and Eileen Heckart.

In the film *A Man Called Horse* starring Richard Harris, during a raid on the Red Indian Yellow Hands Camp one of the braves can be clearly seen wearing sunglasses. In *Knights of the Round Table* starring Robert Taylor and Ava Gardner, in a duel scene a double decker bus can be clearly seen in the background.

Naked Gun 33¹/₃ – the Final Insult is the largest grossing film in cinema history *with a fraction in its title*.

What has *Top Cat* got to do with Schwarzenegger? Well, Arnold Schwarzenegger's surname translates literally as 'black ploughman'. He made his film debut in 1970 with *Hercules In New York* aka *Hercules Goes Bananas* co-starring with Arnold Stang, the man who provided the voice for the title role of the Hanna-Barbera cartoon *Top Cat*.

Film star Mae West was imprisoned for two days in 1927 for writing two plays about prostitutes and transvestites which were performed in New York.

Clarence Nash's impersonation of a baby goat gave Walt Disney the inspiration to create the voice of Donald Duck in 1933. Nash was a talented animal mimic and was employed by the Adhor Milk Company to drive a miniature milk wagon pulled by miniature horses and was billed as Whistling Clarence, the Adhor Bird Man. He specialised in the field of baby chickens, turkeys and crickets but provided Donald's voice for many years after.

David Soul of Starsky and Hutch fame was originally a folk singer who got his first television break wearing a ski mask billed as 'The Covered Man'. He later topped the UK charts without the mask singing 'Don't Give Up On Us' and 'Silver Lady'.

When the BBC televised George VI's coronation in 1937, the scenes were watched by an estimated 10,000 subscribers to the service. Pictures were transmitted from Alexandra Palace relayed by a cable that stretched from the studio to the coronation activity, being unplugged and moved about with the cameras. The BBC sent a Christmas card to all television owners that year.

A ventriloquist's dummy won an Oscar in 1937. Charlie McCarthy, a wooden dummy invented by Edgar Bergen, father of film star Candice Bergen, won it for best comedy creation.

The end credits to the film *The Silence of the Lambs* carry a 'special thanks' for 'Adele, Bobby, and the rest of the gang at Buffa's'. This refers to Oscar winning director Jonathan Demme's penchant for the New York deli Buffa's where he is a regular customer.

In the film *The Doors*, Val Kilmer as Jim Morrison is seen wearing a pair of Ray-Ban 'Wings' sunglasses

Another dummy wins an Oscar.

at a children's party in 1970. Ray-Ban, however, did not introduce the style until 1984. In the same film a conversation takes place in a bar in 1968 regarding the film *Easy Rider*, which was not released until the following year.

Ridley Scott's futuristic 1982 film *Blade Runner* is set in the year 2019 and features advertising and promotion for many American brand names and corporations. However, many of these have failed to survive even into the 90s. They include Pan Am (filed for bankruptcy in 1991); Koss, headphone manufacturers (bankrupt in 1984), and Atari, at that time the top name in the video games market but now a minor player. Also Cuisinart, food processor makers, who went bankrupt in 1989; RCA, which was sold to French and German conglomerates, and Bell systems which was replaced by regional phone companies. *Blade Runner* 'brands' that are still in existence include Coca-Cola, TDK, Schlitz, Budweiser, Jovan and Bulova.

Sadakichi Hartmann appeared on the New York stage in the early 1900s. Billed as a Japanese/German professor his entire act consisted of blowing perfumed smoke at the audience, announcing each aroma to represent a different nation of the world. Hartmann rarely made it to the end of his act, suffering a barrage of heckling and catcalling.

Deep Throat starring Linda Lovelace was the porno film that brought the genre into the mainstream. Filmed for $25,000 in Florida over six days it grossed more than $25 million.

Multi-millionaire eccentric Howard Hughes suffered from chronic constipation. He filled his many hours on the toilet by reading heaps of books and magazines for stories for his films.

'The Woody Woodpecker Song' was nominated for an Oscar in 1948 but lost out to Doris Day's 'Buttons and Bows' from *Annie Get Your Gun*.

The first film to be censored in the UK was Charles Urban's ninety-second film of a piece of Stilton cheese viewed through a microscope. Released in 1898 the image of active bacteria on the cheese created a storm of protest from British cheese makers so it was quietly withdrawn from exhibition.

The British Board of Film Certification censored a scene from the 1990 children's film *Teenage Mutant Ninja Turtles* because it was claimed the turtle named Michelangelo was brandishing a pair of kung fu chainsticks. On closer inspection it was revealed he was in fact swinging a string of sausages but the cut was still enforced.

Daniel Angeli and his partner Jean-Paul Dousset are rated as the kings of the paparazzi for their candid photographs of celebrities caught unaware. They earned an estimated £2 million for their sneak shots of John Bryan sucking the Duchess of York's toes. One man who broke under the pressure of being pursued by these photographic pests was Fiat boss Gianni Agnelli. In order to prevent them continually stalking him he

Howard 'Phews'.

agreed to pose for naked full frontal pictures. After that he was never pursued again.

Top DJ Alan Freeman developed his 'All right stay bright' patter as he signed off when talking to friends on the phone. Actress Ann Todd recommended he used it on his radio show and the rest is history.

The shortest run for a West End play was *The Lady of Lyons* by Lord Lytton which opened on 26 December 1888. The audience was asked to leave after waiting for an hour because nobody could raise the safety curtain. The play was cancelled after that fiasco.

Britain's first DJ was Christopher Stone, brother-in-law of famous writer Compton Mackenzie who originally got the gig but had to take time off for an expedition. Stone made history as he went on the air in BBC studio 3 at Savoy Hill on 7 July 1927, spinning platters and relating personal stories about the records he played. He was not paid but was allowed to give plugs to *Gramophone* magazine which he co-edited with Compton Mackenzie. The BBC soon put a stop to this practice. His future fee was five guineas a session. He recorded his will on a 78 rpm disc in 1931.

If you're anything like me you hate using those cash dispensers, especially the ones that flash up how much you have in your account after giving you the money. Did you know the first automatic cash dispenser in the UK went into action on 27 June 1967 at Barclays Bank,

Enfield. The service was launched by top TV celebrity Reg Varney.

BBC programmes in the 1950s were recorded on VERA – Vision Electronic Recording Apparatus, a machine that used up tape at the rate of ten miles every hour.

The first film in the UK to receive an X certificate was *La Vie Commence Demain*. The 1951 production was considered outrageous because it referred to artificial insemination.

The International Astronomical Union recently named four asteroids in outer space John, Paul, George and Ringo.

Only one man named Oscar has won the treasured Academy Award. He was Oscar Hammerstein II who won two Oscars in the 1940s for lyrics to 'The Last Time I Saw Paris' and 'It Might As Well Be Spring'.

In one of her earliest screen roles Demi Moore was the victim of a flesh-eating monster in the exceedingly bad 1982 film release *Parasite* which was filmed in 3D. *Forrest Gump* star Tom Hanks kick-started his film career in the 1980 slasher release *He Know's You're Alone*. His dinner plans are ruined when his date's head is graphically sliced off, landing in his living room's fish tank.

Tim Jay, a psychology professor at North Adams State College in Massachusetts, studies the use of profanity in American culture. One of his specialist areas is the cinema where he has noted that Eddie Murphy swears every ten seconds in the film *Raw* and that the Al Pacino film *Scarface* uses a swear word every thirty-four seconds. His research has also outlined the five actresses most likely to swear on camera as Whoopi Goldberg, Jane Fonda, Cher, Jodie Foster and Bette Midler.

In the film *Born on the Fourth of July* when Tom Cruise is hospitalised on his return from Vietnam in 1968 Don McLean's hit 'American Pie' can be heard playing in the background. A strange feat as McLean only released the song in 1971.

Sean Connery entered the amateur Mr Universe competition in 1953 and was unplaced.

The rousing march 'Colonel Bogey' was written by Major F. J. Ricketts, bandmaster of the Argyll & Sutherland Highlanders, whilst playing golf in 1913. His opponent continually whistled two warning notes instead of shouting fore! when teeing off and Ricketts could not shake the sounds from his head. He sat down and composed the tune which inspired allied soldiers in two world wars and found everlasting celluloid fame in the 1957 film *The Bridge on the River Kwai*.

In 1976 Elizabeth Taylor was given the accolade 'Most Memorable Eyebrows'. The runner up was Lassie.

Dracula star Bela Lugosi would often become ill and faint at the sight of his own blood.

Lassie concedes victory graciously.

6

FADS AND TRENDS

Public executions in British history were rife with snobbishness. Nobles were beheaded and the working classes hung. Henry VIII's second wife, Anne Boleyn, actually rehearsed her own execution the night before.

Toad-licking became a popular pastime amongst drug users in Australia and the US in the late 1980s. The giant cane toad was found to produce a chemical called bufotenine as a form of defence against its enemies. Humans who licked its head discovered a hallucinogenic property which had the side effects of vomiting and diarrhoea.

Less than 1 per cent of management jobs in Japan are held by women and they are subjected to a list of revealing questions when applying for a job. They are quizzed over whether they are virgins or have boyfriends and are told they stand a better chance if willing to wear mini-skirts. The Japanese Labour Ministry has logged interview questions such as, 'Please show me the side of your face, you have a lot of make up on,' and, 'We want women who have beautiful legs.'

Flagpole-sitting was a popular fad throughout the US in the 1920s. Originated by Alvin Kelly, who used the name Shipwreck, the craze spread like wildfire coast to coast.

His original squat of thirteen hours and thirteen minutes in Los Angeles led to a forty-nine-day session in Atlantic City watched by over 20,000 people. Alvin was later hospitalised with a condition known as flagpole anus – ooh!

Frisbees originated in the nineteenth century as the tin dish used to bake pies on by the Frisbie Pie Company in Bridgeport, Connecticut. Local students at Yale University discovered, after consuming their lunch, that the dishes had amazing aerodynamic qualities when thrown to each other. In 1948 building inspector Fred Morrison modified the dish in plastic and named it 'Morrison's Flying Saucer'. He later sold the rights to the Wham-O Corporation (inventors of the Hula-hoop) who sold it around the world as the Frisbee at the same time the Frisbie Bakery went out of business.

Children over the centuries have always enjoyed ringing doorbells and then running away, breaking the law according to the Town Police Causes Act of 1847. There are over sixty different names for the activity throughout the UK. In the south it's known as 'Knock Down Ginger', in Scotland 'Cheeky Nellie' and in the Lake District 'Tappit'. Wales has 'Cherry Knocking' whilst Manchester enjoys 'White Rabbit'.

In 1962 the House of Commons enjoyed heated exchanges when an opposition spokesman claimed that the Tory Health Minister, Enoch Powell, had been involved in 'activities unbecoming a Greek scholar and gentleman'. Mr Powell's crime? He had been spotted bouncing around on a pogo stick in Eaton Square, London.

Don't try this at home folks.

Popular fads of the 1970s included *The Nothing Book*, a volume consisting entirely of blank pages; pet rocks, lumps of rock sold at $5 a time; and bottle money, worthless shredded banknotes contained in large jars.

Loon pants originated in the 1960s when demand for bell bottoms exceeded supply. The Laurence Corner Army Surplus Store in London began to sell summer-weight, naval-issue bell bottoms which they altered by narrowing the thighs and lowering the waist. They were sold by mail order as loon pants, the name derived from the hippie phrase 'looning about' literally meaning to disport oneself in an uninhibited manner.

When the streaking phenomenon hit its peak in 1974 US TV companies utilised guards at all live sporting events to prevent naked spectators coming in to view of the cameras. The appearance of streakers from behind bushes at golf championships was particularly prevalent. Streakers appeared at the Oscars, the Johnny Carson TV Show, during a Nureyev ballet and at top classical concerts. An elderly man and woman were arrested for 'snailing' as they were streaking so slowly.

Afro hairstyles were banned in Tanzania in the 1960s because they were seen as symbols of neo-coloniasim. Black activist George Jackson was shot in San Quentin jail in the US by guards who were convinced he was hiding a pistol in his bushy afro.

Dance marathons were popular throughout the US in the 1930s. Contestants were usually allowed fifteen minutes rest

Zimmer Strippers.

in each three hour period. The longest contest recorded ran for 3,780 hours or 158 days.

The UK's first holiday camp was Dodd's Socialist Holiday Camp at Caister-On-Sea, Norfolk, which opened its doors in 1906. Alcohol was banned and holidaymakers talking after 11 p.m. were evicted from the premises. 'Rowdy and improper language' was banned and a fine of 6d imposed if a tent was not kept tidy.

Dutch mystic Dr Bart Hughes declared in 1962 that having a hole drilled through the cranium enabled people to reach a higher state of consciousness. The operation was known as trepanning. Dr Hughes was committed to a mental hospital but visited the UK in 1966 to spread his ideas. He was extradited from the country by the Home Office and banned as an undesirable alien.

Goldfish swallowing was popular in US colleges shortly before World War II. A student at Kutztown State Teacher's College, Reading, Pennsylvania, managed to down forty-three in one session. The craze later extended to eating 78 rpm records and magazines.

The Hula-hoop was launched in the US in 1958 by Wham-O Corporation and sold thirty million within six months. Their product the Limbo Bar appeared on the market in 1962 but was a complete flop.

Peter Adolph invented the table football game Subbuteo in 1947. A keen bird watcher, he wanted to call it 'The Hobby' after his favourite bird but was not allowed to because the name was defined as descriptive. He substituted the latin name instead, *Falco subbuteo subbuteo* – The Hobby Bird.

Pantie raids took place in US colleges throughout the 1950s. Male students would invade female dormitories in the middle of the night to collect as much lingerie as possible. The craze caught on rapidly with many females initiating underpants raids in reprisal.

Yoyos were first commercially produced by Chicago toy maker Donald Duncan in 1929. He had seen the game played in the Phillipines where yoyo's literally translated as 'come come'.

The word 'chauvinism' derives from a French soldier named Nicholas Chauvin who praised Napoleon continuously. His name became associated with those who were violently devoted to a nation or group. Only recently has it been applied to sexual groups.

Crew cuts originated from the hairstyle enjoyed by US college rowing teams in the 1930s.

Scoobidoos were popular in schools in the UK and US in the 1960s. Enjoyed by both boys and girls, the Scoobidoo consisted of strips of coloured plastic which were laced to produce key fobs and watchstraps. They originated in France as the 'scoubidou'.

Mad hatters were common in the eighteenth century because hat makers used mercury to process beaver and rabbit fur and many succumbed to mercury poisoning. The disease gave all the appearances of lunacy beginning with the shakes followed by mental aberrations.

In the 1960s straight hair was so popular among girls that many ironed their locks an inch at a time to achieve the perfect look.

The phrase 'the real McCoy' stems from US boxer Charles 'Kid' McCoy, a welterweight champion who was unbeaten in his class. However, he accidentally killed his lover in a tiff and was sentenced to prison. During his period in jail he saved the life of a pilot who crashed his plane near where McCoy was working on a chain gang. His fame increased throughout the US and his name began to be applied to anything that was thought 'the real thing'. McCoy died of a sleeping pill overdose in 1940.

In the 1920s hip black Americans had their hair straightened using a product called Congolene. When applied to the hair the finished effect was known as a 'conk'. This hairstyle has been used by both Michael Jackson and Prince.

Hush Puppies are always associated with suede shoes but in the southern US states Hush Puppies are a corn meal batter served with fried fish. They are a popular meal given to dogs.

The Wham-O Corporation launched the 'Super Ball' in the US in the 1960s. The concentrated black rubber sphere would bounce at crazy angles and could bounce for one

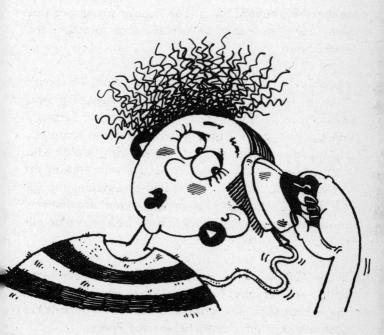

'Sorry – I'm ironing my hair tonight.'

minute if thrown correctly. Lamar Hunt, oil tycoon and US football team owner, was searching for a name for a championship match between the AFL and the NFL and was inspired to call it the Superbowl after watching his son play with his Super Ball.

7
FOOD AND EATING

Drambuie liqueur was invented by the family of Bonnie Prince Charlie and kept a secret for generations. When the prince was defeated after the battle of Culloden in 1745 he was given refuge on the Isle of Skye by a Captain John Mackinnon to whom he gave the secret formula. It was a strong alcoholic drink called *buidhe* meaning pleasing. The secret remained with the Mackinnon family until the early twentieth century when they began to produce it commercially. The formula is still the same and the chairman's wife is still traditionally required to prepare the drink's secret ingredients.

In May 1968 the University of Colorado student body named the grill room of their cafeteria the 'Alfred Packer Grill' in honour of the only American ever to be convicted of cannibalism. In 1874 Packer had admitted eating his companions on a trek across the Rockies after a fellow traveller Shannon Wilson Bell had killed the other members of their group and he had then killed Bell in self-defence. He turned to cannibalism when the temperature plummeted to $-50°$ F. He died a free man in 1907 after seventeen years in prison.

The world's first self-service store or supermarket was the Piggly Wiggly store which opened in Memphis, Tennessee in 1916. Within ten years there were over 3,000 Piggly Wigglys across the US. The Co-Op gave the

UK its first supermarket with Tesco closely following in the 1940s with their St Albans store. That store later reverted back from self-service because of the high incidence of theft.

Britain's first curry house was the Salut-e-Hind which opened its doors in Holborn in 1911. There are now over 7,500 Indian restaurants in the UK and London now has more curry houses than Delhi.

The Edwardian music hall song 'Let's All Go Down the Strand' is still popular today and is always sung with the phrase 'Have a banana'. This line was not written in the original version but added by the chief salesman of banana importers Elders & Fyffes, namely Roger Ackerly. It guaranteed instant promotion of the fruit whenever the song was sung.

Nestlé invented instant coffee in the 1930s after a glut of coffee beans in South America filled up all available storage space and more room was needed for the next harvest.

Hovis bread takes its name from the Latin phrase '*Hominis vis*' literally translating as 'Strength of man'.

To improve the image of slaughterhouses in Great Britain the French word *abattoir* was adopted instead. It literally means that something or somebody has been knocked off or beaten down.

Sales of fish fingers in the UK now average £100-million-worth a year but when Bird's Eye first launched them in this country in the 1950s they were branded as 'the herring savoury'.

The slogan 'Come alive with Pepsi' was translated in Germany as 'Come alive out of the grave with Pepsi'. In some Slavic countries it has been translated as 'Pepsi brings your ancestors back from the grave'.

Colonel Sanders first produced his legendary fried chicken recipe at his small restaurant and petrol station in Corbin, Kentucky in the 1930s. His recipe containing eleven different herbs and spices was a success but he later sold up and quit because his business was running at a loss. He later cooked his chicken dish for restaurateur Leon Harman who was so impressed he bought the recipe and the name and sold the franchise worldwide. By the 1960s the business was turning over $37 million a year.

Japanese sushi bars that serve raw fish are now common all over the western world. One of the most deadly varieties of sushi is the puffer or fugu fish. Eaten raw it is highly poisonous and can kill an unsuspecting diner if not prepared properly by an expert chef. Some Japanese chefs leave just enough poison in the flesh to allow a diner's lips to tingle so they know how close they are to mortality. One shred of its deadly flesh that could fit under a man's fingernail could be enough to wipe out an entire family.

Ray Kroc is famed as the man who developed the McDonald's chain of restaurants but he originally started out as the owner of the Multimixer Milk Machine Company. His machines were installed at the burger bars across California of brothers Richard and Maurice McDonald. Kroc was constantly amazed at their standard of speed and service and the custom they attracted. The McDonalds had no interest in expanding elsewhere and sold Kroc the franchise rights, the name and concept for $2.7 million in 1961. By September 1990 the company had sold its eighty billionth burger, opening a branch every four hours. There is now a McDonald's at the South Pole and 145 of their hamburgers are consumed worldwide every second of the day.

Drinking a toast at a formal occasion derives from early Greece where the host at a gathering would sip his drink first to prove that it was not poisoned. The Romans adopted the custom adding toasted bread to their wine to reduce its acidity.

Crisps are manufactured so they cannot be eaten whole. This allows the consumer to enjoy the satisfaction of hearing them crackle when eaten as the mouth has to remain open. Does anyone know what happened to Bovril crisps?

It was common in eighteenth-century Britain to torture animals before killing them in the mistaken belief it improved their taste in the cooking process. Many were suspended upside down and allowed to bleed to death whilst pigs and calves were often whipped to death.

Christian Nelson invented choc ices at his sweet shop in

Iowa, USA, in 1921. A young boy had entered his premises and could not decide whether to spend his pocket money on chocolate or ice cream. Nelson came up with the idea of a mixture of both and named it Eskimo pie.

The asparagus has a strong acid element which in many people creates a pungent odour in their urine. In olden times when chamber pots were in common use asparagus was referred to as 'chambermaids horror'. The University of Birmingham recently surveyed the urine found in 800 asparagus eaters and discovered almost 50 per cent produced the sickly sweet scent.

Percy Spencer invented the microwave oven by accident during World War II when manufacturing radar equipment. He regularly used magnetrons to heat his hands during the winter but one day noticed they had melted a sweet in his pocket. He soon perfected a cooking process which he submitted to the board of directors of his company. He demonstrated his invention to them with an egg which promptly exploded but he was still given the green light for development.

Stir frying and chopsticks originated in the Chinese Chou dynasty when the country faced a fuel shortage. The speedy method of stir frying was used to conserve energy. With tables also a rarity one hand had to be free to hold the bowl and thus chopsticks were invented.

The most recognised brand of packaged food in the world is Spam, a subtle combination of pork and ham. The staple diet of servicemen in the twentieth century it was not used in the Gulf War at the request of the Saudi authorities who objected to its pork content.

In Hong Kong waiters sprinkle starchy white tablecloths with tea before diners sit down so they can avoid the embarrassment of spilling food during their meal.

Aristophanes' play *The Ecclesiazusae* refers to a goulash made up of left-over meals. It is described as: Lopadotemachoselachogaleokranioleipsanodrimhypotrimmatosilphioparaomelitokatakechymenokichlepikossyphophattoperisteralektryonoptekephalliokigklopeleiolagoiosiraiobaphetraganopterygon. It's quicker to eat than spell it.

Tea is consumed in Tibet by mixing it with rancid yak milk and churning it until it forms a thick soup-like substance.

Ice cream sundaes were invented in the town of Evanston, Illinois, in the late nineteenth century because of a religious ban that did not allow the serving of ice cream with soda on the Sabbath. Shopkeepers got round it by serving ice cream with syrup instead and called them 'Sundays'. Over the years the name developed into sundae.

Hiram Cod invented a gas-tight bottle in the 1870s to preserve the fizz in lemonade. Wallop was a slang term for beer and because it was never kept in a Cod bottle the phrase 'Cod's wallop' was used to describe a drink that was non-alcoholic.

In the US the Public Health Service of the Food and Drug Administration publishes a list of defect levels which are not to be exceeded if the food is to be sold for human consumption. All the following are acceptable under the code for the American public. Coffee beans are acceptable if only 10 per cent insect infested, damaged or moulded and 100-gram samples of spinach are okay if they contain no more than either fifty aphids, thrips or mites or eight leaf miners, two spinach worms or 10 per cent decomposition. . . . In a 100-gram sample of tomato paste either 30 fly eggs, 15 eggs and one larvae, or two larva or mould count averaging 40 per cent (30 per cent for pizza sauce).

Soybeans cause the highest levels of flatulence amongst pulses claims a survey by Dr Louis B. Rockland of the Western Regional Research Laboratory at the US Department of Agriculture in Berkeley, California. The beans take effect within four hours of consumption and Dr Rockland recommends cooking soybeans with rice which can cut the farts down by two thirds.

When dining out in a Rumanian restaurant don't be too worried about seeing crap on the menu. Its the Rumanian word for carp.

8

HAGS IN HISTORY

Hungarian King Matthias Corvinus insisted that all ladies in his court remained seated in his presence as he considered them all extremely ugly.

In the book *Shropshire Folklore* by Charlotte Burne published in 1883 the story of Priss Morris is told. She lived in the Cleobury North area and was able at will to make horses immobile despite any efforts made by their riders.

Some witches moved around appearing and disappearing using a 'Hand of Glory'. The hand taken, from a hanged man, was pickled and given a satanic baptism. If a lit candle was placed in the hand it was claimed anyone in the vicinity would fall asleep.

A bill was presented to parliament in 1770 which demanded that any woman should not seduce or betray into matrimony any of his majesty's subjects. It set out to ban the use of 'scents, paints, cosmetic washes, artificial teeth, false hair, Spanish wool, iron stays, hoops, high heeled shoes'. If any of these were used to entice a man into marriage the woman would incur 'the penalty of the law in force against witchcraft and like misdemeanours and the marriage upon conviction shall stand null and void'. The bill was defeated.

In 1978 the US army issued orders that all service chaplains be willing and able to minister to the increasing number of service personnel who were witches.

Witchcraft was still a criminal offence in Britain until 1951. The Witchcraft Act of 1736 was replaced by the Fraudulent Mediums Act. A Mrs Helen Duncan was arrested and tried at the Old Bailey under this act as recently as 1944 when the police raided the Master Temple Psychic Centre above a shop in Portsmouth. She received a nine-month jail sentence for using a cloth to emulate a spirit at a seance. She had been previously prosecuted in 1933 for ripping a vest under her dress to create the sound of an unearthly spirit.

Contrary to evidence from frescoes unearthed from the ruined city of Pompeii which was destroyed by the eruption of Vesuvius in 79 AD, the women of that city were not as beautiful as historians used to think. The myth, perpetuated in Frankie Howerd's TV series *Up Pompeii*, portrayed the womenfolk as archetypes of classic beauty. However, scientists now claim they were obese, hairy, unhealthy and affected by a hormonal disorder commonly associated with post-menopausal women.

In 1722 an old woman in Scotland was burnt to death after being convicted of turning her daughter into a pony and riding her to a witches' coven.

Britain's witchcraft laws were the mildest in Europe. The Witchcraft Act of 1736 forbade torture and only allowed a sentence of death on those guilty of murder by sorcery.

A nineteenth-century bridegroom sued his father-in-law for deception after his wife removed her make up the morning after their wedding. He filed suit claiming compensation 'suitable to her real and not her assumed countenance'. He told the court he never realized until daylight came what a hag he had chosen for a spouse.

When sex testing was first introduced at the 1966 European Athletic Championships in Budapest a record number of Eastern European competitors mysteriously dropped out before the testing began.

Medieval witches drummed up business by telling women that pregnancy pains were caused by kittens in their womb. They sold potions to ease the pain. Hence the the phrase 'to have kittens', meaning to be anxious or afraid.

Witches were said to strip naked before broomstick flights and coat their bodies and broomstick with a flying ointment. Their preferred take-off route was up the chimney but they had to beware of church bells which could immediately ground their flight.

It is estimated that over one million witches were executed worldwide in the Middle Ages.

In medieval times witches celebrated Walpurgis Night and Halloween at a variety of venues in Europe. Meetings could be found at La Hendaye in France,

A little in-flight turbulence.

Germany's Haaz Mountains and the Blakulla Plain in Sweden. Attendances of over 12,000 were not uncommon.

In Polish legend a witch called Pszepolnica roams the countryside beheading any person who cannot talk about flax for one hour or more.

One of the commonest tests for a woman accused of witchcraft in olden times was to tie her right thumb to her left big toe and then throw her into a pond or river. If she floated she was deemed to be a witch. A German archbishop in the ninth century revised the process adding a rope so the woman could be saved if she did sink. It was believed that witches refused to go near baptismal water, as the water would reject them.

In Britain in the Middle Ages three signs were often used in witch hunting: testing to see if a woman could not weep more than three tears only from the left eye, repeating the Lord's prayer without error and seeing if they weighed less than a church bible. Failing any of these could lead to condemnation as a witch.

9
TELEVISION

St Clare Of Assisi was proclaimed by the Pope to be the patron saint of television in 1959. She was a thirteenth-century nun who once prayed on her sick bed so that she could see a vision of a Christmas Eve church service that she could not attend. She witnessed the full service in her room and the Pope saw this as an antecedent of 'the modern miracle of television'.

The theme to top detective series *Inspector Morse* contains the morse code equivalent of the letters M O R S E.

If you think British sitcoms are bad just sample some of these plot lines from these US shows.

Bungle Abbey – The wacky adventures of a bunch of fun loving monks.
Happy – A hotel manager discovers his baby can talk like an adult (or even Mr Ed) and spends each episode keeping his secret from the guests.
It's About Time – Two astronauts fly into the past by accident and return to modern day New York with a feuding Stone Age couple.
Mixed Nuts – Comic escapades of doctors, nurses and inmates at a lunatic asylum.
My Living Doll – Psychiatrist lives with a 37–26–36 female robot

who performs household tasks and can be reprogrammed if she answers back.

My Mother the Car – Man buys a car only to discover it is the reincarnation of his dead mother.

The Second Hundred Years – A prospector from the Alaskan gold rush is frozen in a block of ice and wakes up in modern day America.

Struck By Lightning – Dr Victor Frankenstein runs a small hotel in Maine with his monster creation as his handyman.

The Ugliest Girl In Town – Man dressed as a woman becomes a top model in London.

One of America's weirdest TV shows was the *$1.98 Beauty Show* which featured strange-looking people parading as if competing for the Miss World title. Winners were given a tinsel crown, a bouquet of withered carrots and $1.98 in prize money.

The Professionals starring Gordon Jackson, Martin Shaw and Lewis Collins as agents for the mysterious (and fictitious) CI5 was one of British TV's most successful exports and was seen around the world. In 1984 Libyans surrounded the British Embassy in Tripoli in a demonstration over the Libyan People's Bureau siege and their favourite chant was 'Down with CI5'.

I've always been a fan of US TV movies which in most cases are made on the most minimal budget possible. My favourite era is the 1970s where everything looks really cheap and men wore shirt collars big enough to take your eye out. The following are all real TV movies that were shown on US television.

'And I'd like to work with animals and children . . .'

Someone I Touched – A man and a woman fight over who gave them herpes.

The Beasts are on the Street – Exotic marauding animals take over a small US town after a car accident destroys the fence of a local safari park.

Beg, Borrow ... or Steal – Three men, one legless, one with one eye and one handless, join forces to steal museum treasures.

The Feminist and the Fuzz – A women's liberationist is forced to become a roommate with a macho, male chauvinist cop.

Kiss Meets the Phantom of the Park – Rock group Kiss fight a mad scientist who has built Kiss robots.

Mars Needs Women – Aliens send out signals to Earth that they need female company.

US TV has always borrowed heavily from the movies and once a film has become a box office success you can be sure there'll be a small-screen version. Here are some that didn't quite become hits.

Bates' Motel – *Psycho* spin-off where mad killer inherits the infamous motel.

Butch Cassidy and the Sundance Kids – Dropping the Western theme cartoon teens go undercover for the FBI as the world's greatest rock band.

The Oddball Couple – Cartoon version of the comedy classic *The Odd Couple* with Fleabag the dog and Spiffy the cat.

In 1963 cartoon Beatles were used to advertise Nestlé's Jellimallo bars on TV. Not to be outdone the Rolling

Stones provided the music for a Rice Krispies advert which was a parody of top pop show *Juke Box Jury*.

Comedian Dave Allen was the original choice to play Jeff Randall in the TV series *Randall and Hopkirk*. The role was eventually played by Mike Pratt.

Top Irish comedian Dave Allen was born David Tynan O'Mahoney. He first found TV fame in Australia in the 1960s with his chat show *Tonight With Dave Allen*. The programme achieved notoriety when Allen interviewed Peter Cook and Dudley Moore and was frantically signalled to wrap up his conversation by a flustered floor manager. Allen turned to him live on air and told him to 'go away and masturbate'.

Hugh Laurie of Fry and Laurie comic fame was a member of the 1980 Cambridge Boat Race team who lost to Oxford.

During a dance routine at the 1963 Royal Variety Performance pint-sized comic Charlie Drake stopped in mid-act and addressed the royal box. He said, 'I was so pleased to see your horse won at Kempton, Your Majesty,' and then carried on with his act.

In 1979 ITV went off the air for seventy-five days when technicians went on strike. Research showed that an estimated one million viewers kept their TV permanently on ITV during the period, viewing a blank screen in the hope the channel would reappear.

John Logie Baird made the world's first television

transmission above a shop in Hastings in 1924. He constructed a receiver from an old electric motor, a tea chest, a biscuit tin, cardboard, piano wire, string, sealing wax, glue, a cycle lamp lens and some needles.

The Russian communist newspaper *Pravda* warned TV viewers in the 1960s not to watch *Batman* because 'he is nothing more than a glorified FBI agent, a capitalist murderer who kills his enemies beautifully, effectively, and with taste, so that shoulder blades crack loudly and scalps break like cantaloupes'.

On 29 July 1981 an estimated TV audience of 750 million worldwide watched the wedding of Prince Charles and Lady Diana Spencer. In Great Britain alone the audience was measured at 39 million, an all-time record. BBC engineers introduced a system that day called ISLA (Instant Substituting from Live Action) which provided a service for the deaf on screen, printing up commentator Tom Fleming's words as he spoke them. Three keyboard operators instantly typed his sombre tones phonetically into a microcomputer which was supposed to match the phonetic signal with the word that came closest to it. In principle the system should have worked a treat but viewers with the facility to receive the subtitles saw the message, 'Princess Anne is wearing an a masing outfit. Very sump. Shs flat a big frill down the sid.' The wacky messages continued: 'Lady Dja na foamed out of the glass coach wearing hundreds of jarts of veil, a tiny bodies and a gate big skirt. Prince Charles (the air to the throne) ascended the Redcar pet with the dew of Edinburgh. The Queen clad in cre D sheen sparkling with qui stls and saphires carried a handbag in which eyed think today there might be a po ct handkerchief.' 'Bride and groom left St Pauls through a csea of hugh man faces to the sound of wringing bells.'

Britain's first domestic satellite dish went on sale in 1981. Manufactured in Sweden the two-metre in diameter dish cost an astounding £5,000.

When *Dad's Army* was originally planned John Le Mesurier was cast as pompous bank manager Captain Mainwaring whilst Arthur Lowe was set to play the wimpish Sergeant Wilson. Before the series went on air however they reversed their roles to create two of TV's most enduring comic characters.

These shows all appeared on US TV: *Partridge Family – 2200 A.D.*, *The New Odd Couple* (with a black Felix and Oscar), *The Beverly Hillbillies Solve the Energy Crisis*, *David Cassidy – Man Undercover*, *The Brady Bunch Variety Hour* and who could forget *Look What's Happened To Rosemary's Baby*.

A TV licence cost just £2 in 1946.

In the Classic 'Germans' episode of *Fawlty Towers* disaster-prone waiter Manuel sets himself on fire in the kitchen. When this episode was being filmed actor Andrew Sachs really did set himself on fire and later received £700 in compensation from the BBC.

The Newlyweds Game debuted on US TV in January 1967. Four couples who had been married for less than a year answered questions about each other while the other partner sat in a sound-proof booth. They then had to guess what the answers were. The format was later adopted here for *Mr & Mrs*. The series became essential viewing in the US when compere Bob Eubanks asked a couple, 'Where will your husband say is the strangest place the two of you have ever made whoopee?' The woman replied, 'In the butt, Bob.'

In 1979 a two-year study of US children between the ages of four and eight was made about their TV viewing habits. When asked who they preferred, TV or daddy? 44 per cent said they preferred TV.

John Ryan who created, wrote and drew the classic children's TV series *Captain Pugwash* received a measly £4 from the BBC when he supplied them with a pilot episode.

10
HEALTH

As listeners to my radio shows may know I'm a hypochondriac, so this health section is of particular interest to me. Let's start with a smell I love: TCP is one of the most used antiseptics in households across the world but it was originally formulated as a bacterial antiseptic to combat VD.

On 15 August 1951 the entire population of the French village of Point San Espirit was declared collectively mad. One in twenty of the 4,000 inhabitants suffered vomiting, delirium, hallucinations, insomnia and a burning sensation in the anus. Four later died. The disease was known as St Anthony's Fire and was caused by eating bread made from 'smutty rye' which contained a poisonous fungus. The illness was a common malady in mediaeval times.

The number of suicides in the UK has dropped by 20 per cent in the past thirty years. This is thought to be due to the success of the Samaritans but also because of the switch to North Sea gas.

Painter Pablo Picasso was abandoned at birth as stillborn by a midwife but was revived by his uncle who blew cigar smoke into his lungs.

In 1977 a nineteenth-month-old baby from Qatar's life

was saved at Hammersmith Hospital, London because a nurse was reading an Agatha Christie thriller. Doctors were at a loss to diagnose the child's condition until the nurse who was reading *The Pale Horse* by Britain's 'Queen of Crime' recognised the symptoms of thallium poisoning which featured in the book. The child responded to treatment and made a full recovery.

The Royal College of Physicians estimate that one fifth of British death certificates are incorrect, the cause of death being given wrongly.

The Gesundheit Institute in Arlington, Virginia is a medical centre run in the belief that humour is the best medicine. The principal, Hunter Adams MD, believes in training doctors to be happy and fun loving with patients and to inject jokes into the medical world.

Politician and statesman Sir Winston Churchill was born in a ladies' cloakroom at his family's ancestral home, Blenheim Palace, after his mother went into labour during a ball there.

The peak 60-minute period for heart attacks in the UK is between 8 a.m. and 9 a.m on Monday mornings.

Research in the US has shown that when women live together in groups their menstrual cycles become synchronised: 127 female college students who lived in a group of 12 houses surrounding a courtyard were monitored when they began their autumn term. The first month showed an average of up to 13.7 days difference between each woman's period in the group which reduced to 2.6 days by the second month.

Pneumonoultramicroscopicsilicovolcanoconiosis is a disease common in miners who inhale silicate or quartz dust.

Nineteenth-century surgeon Robert Liston was known as the fastest knife in the West End. He invented sticking plaster, the 'Bulldog' artery forceps and a leg splint that was still in use during World War II. He performed the first operation under anaesthetic in Europe in 1846, amputating a leg in under two-and-a-half minutes. His errors, however, were also legendary. He once removed a patient's testicles by mistake during a leg amputation and in one operation he removed the fingers of an assistant who later died from gangrene poisoning. One of his fastest operations was the removal of a 45-pound scrotal tumour from a patient who carried the enlarged parts in a wheelbarrow.

One of the largest items left in a human body after an operation was a set of forceps measuring seven and a half inches by three inches. They were discovered in the ashes of a 76-year-old woman a week after a kidney operation. The wound had measured seven inches by three and a half inches after the surgery and could never have concealed the forceps. No instruments were found to be missing from the operating theatre at the time.

Charles II was famous for giving 'the royal touch' during his reign to cure a disease called 'the king's evil'. This was a disease called scrofula — swollen, tuberculous glands in the neck. He performed a touching ceremony in front of

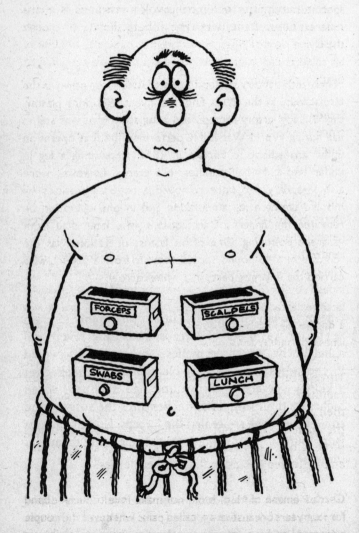

Forensic filing.

spectators complete with the music of massed choirs where sufferers believed they were being touched by God through the divine right of kings. He laid hands on almost 100,000 of his subjects and in one session six people were trampled to death in the rush to be cured by the king.

Beachy Head in Sussex has been a popular suicide site since the sixth century. At the 532-foot drop July and August are the most popular months with Friday the favourite day.

On 14 August 1922 forty-four guests of the Loch Maree Hotel in Scotland set out on a fishing trip with a packed lunch prepared by the hotel containing wild duck potted meat sandwiches. All suffered severe food poisoning and eight died. The paste had been tainted in the can and the whole canning industry suffered a drastic downturn in trade. Insurers Lloyds later instigated a policy offering £1,000 cover for half a crown a bed to all hotels and boarding houses covering them for illness caused by food poisoning.

Three hundred years ago male gynaecologists were required to enter an expectant woman's bedroom on their hands and knees to perform an examination so the patient could not see the owner of the fingers probing her. They regularly worked in darkened rooms and delivered babies under the bedclothes.

Gerda Piemann of Munich did not make love to her husband for four years because of agonising pains whenever the couple attempted to have sex. After a medical examination it was revealed that she had an inch-long shard of a surgeon's needle inside her which had been left behind after a minor bladder operation. Gerda is now suing the surgeon involved for £6,000 for the pain and the interruption to her sex life.

Musical epilepsy is a disease where sufferers constantly replay songs in their head. One patient registered continuous replays of 'The Green Shamrock of Ireland' whilst another was subjected to a loop medley of 'Daisy, Daisy', 'Let Me Call You Sweetheart', 'After The Ball Is Over' and 'Nearer My God To Thee'.

The first blood transfusions took place as long ago as the seventeenth century using blood from cows sheep but were not a success. The first voluntary donor service began in the UK in 1924 with just twenty-six requests for blood from hospitals.

A Pictorial Book of Tongue Coating was published in Japan in 1981. Diagnosis by looking at the tongue is an ancient oriental method of analysing illness and the book provides 257 full colour photographs of people with their tongues out. Highlights include plate 63: Pink tongue with red spots, purple speckles and thin whitish greasy fur; plate 196: Deep red tongue with a slippery moist 'mouldy sauce paste' fur and plate 217: Bluish purple lean small tongue with a white rotten fur.

When US President James Garfield was shot in 1881 surgeons used a metal detecting machine to hunt for the bullet lodged somewhere in his body. The early prototype of a machine that is now found in airports worldwide had been created by the inventor of the telephone, Alexander Graham Bell.

Plate 63: Pink tongue with red spots, purple specks
and thin whitish greasy fur.

But it could not save the President. Interference from the bedsprings sent the machine haywire and he died from his wounds.

A trip to the barbers in Yemen can provide more than a haircut. Circumcisions to order can also be supplied on the premises.

The US National Institute of Medicine estimates that three quarters of Americans die as a result of their lifestyle, factors ranging from smoking, drinking, violence and drugs to stress.

Cystitis amongst women increased in the 1960s when short skirts and tights replaced stockings. The tight constriction of nylon in the crotch area led to infection by retaining moisture and heat whilst excluding air. Research conducted by the clothing industry also discovered that women were urinating less frequently because of the amount of time it took to rearrange their clothes after using the lavatory.

Residents of some rural parts of Europe still believe that asthma can be cured by eating cats or licking the foam from a mule's mouth.

Robert Cheeseborough invented vaseline in the nineteenth century after noticing oil field workers eased cuts and burns with the residue that collected on the rods of drilling rigs. He lived until the age of ninety-six, consuming a spoonful of the product he invented each day.

A popular cure for ear trouble in the world of alternative medicine is the Hopi ear candle as used by Native American Indians. The candle is stuck in the ear and ignited and acts like a chimney sucking out impurities such as wax. It has been found to be useful for all ear problems ranging from tinnitus to glue ear.

Healing the hard of hearing – the Hopi way.

11

HUMAN BEHAVIOUR

What we do and how we do it, idiosyncrasies, habits and our weird ways are listed in this section.

Accidents in public places in Japan are growing with at least twenty-four fatalities in Tokyo alone in the last five years. The deaths and injuries are being caused by the Oriental habit of bowing when meeting people for the first time. As this often takes place in business situations at railway stations and airports many people have been nudged in front of trains, knocked down escalators and trapped in revolving doors. Authorities are now planning to install greeting zones in hazardous areas.

Touching the ear is an insult in Italy which says you are a homosexual and should wear an earring.

Many adults rock on the balls of their feet before giving speeches or taking part in events with an audience. This is thought to be a comforting movement reaching right back to life as a baby when a mother would rock her child to sleep.

Males in New Guinea tribes place foot-long tubes over their penises before going to war as a display of male dominance. With an average length of 6¼ inches the penis is less than one tenth the height of an adult male. Many phallic statues from ancient civilisations have been found to be over 200 feet high.

Studies show that touching a stranger when making a request results in more social influence. Market researchers or petitioners are far more likely to get a result by touching someone in the street rather than making just a verbal approach.

A row of Xs at the bottom of a letter represented 'Saint Andrew's Mark' when first used in the Middle Ages. Saint Andrew was martyred on an X-shaped cross and this symbol represented a promise to be honest in his sacred name. A letter writer would then kiss the Xs before sending the note to its intended recipient, thus turning the cross into the representation of a kiss.

In many Mediterranean countries the sign for hitchhiking, an upraised thumb, is an insult meaning 'sit on this'.

Holding the hand of the elderly and the ill apart from giving emotional strength can also lower their blood pressure.

Giving the index finger is a gesture that dates from Roman times. It was known then as the 'infamous' or 'obscene' digit.

Researchers who observed people in public places concluded that males touch females first; females are more likely to touch females than males are to touch males

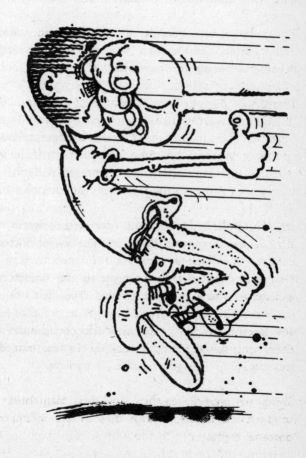

Something's lost in the translation.

and that people with higher positions in life tend to touch those of a lower order first. Lower-status citizens wait for a signal before touching their superiors.

The waltz was once considered the most degenerate dance ever invented. The Victorian *Ladies' Pocket Book of Etiquette* devoted ten pages into denouncing it.

The V sign derives from the battle of Agincourt when the French warned British archers they would cut off their first and second fingers (the bow fingers) if caught. Henry V warned his men of their intent inspiring them to victory which they celebrated with the now infamous gesture to their defeated opponents.

Sir Winston Churchill's famous V for Victory sign in World War II was originated by a Belgian. Lawyer Victor De Lavelaye saw members of the resistance daubing walls with the slogan RAF and suggested the briefer V for victory was perhaps more suitable. The idea was taken up by the BBC who prefaced messages to occupied Europe with Beethoven's 5th Symphony which contained the morse code signal for V. Churchill took up the idea immediately and the upraised fingers became his trademark.

When people tell lies they tend to gesticulate less. An unconscious sense reminds us that if hands are used the actions may not fit the words. Politicians are adept at lying with body language.

A survey in US restaurants discovered that waitresses who unobtrusively touched diners gained larger tips.

The ring sign indicates OK in the US, zero in France, money in Japan, and is an obscenity in the Middle East.

Researchers deliberately left a coin in a public phone box and then asked the next customer if they had found it. By touching the person it was found that the chances of receiving the coin back were boosted from 63 per cent to 96 per cent.

When people first meet there is a subconscious period during which their speech patterns synchronise. To compensate, non-verbal signals, nods and shifts of gaze are used.

In Greece, the 'Moutza', a gesture placing the palm near the face, derives from the habit of throwing dirt in criminal's faces as they were led through the streets. The fingers and thumbs splayed were said to indicate the five worse sexual practices that could be inflicted on female relatives.

Though still prevalent today only in front of royalty, bowing and curtsying survived in the UK until the nineteenth century but began to disappear when social life grew more complex and the population increased. It was gradually replaced by the more simple handshake.

The 'fig sign' is still common and dates back to the earliest era of history. It involves squeezing the thumb between the first two fingers with just the tip showing. It derives from the idea that exposing the genitals to evil spirits would divert their attention. The sign appeared on carvings in many Christian churches.

Mankind is safer now from natural hazards than his ancestors ever were but the acute reflex of panic is still present, especially noticeable in dense crowds when a sudden movement can spark off a chain reaction.

Sir Robert Baden-Powell, founder of the Boy Scout movement, was convinced he could analyse any person's character by the way they walked. He claimed that 50 per cent of women were adventurous with one leg but more hesitant with the other which indicated that they were liable to act on impulse. He also thought that anyone walking with their toes turned out was in all probability a liar. He met up with his wife whilst admiring her distinctive strides onboard a ship (claiming later that he had first spotted her two years before walking in Knightsbridge and had made a mental note about her). He published a book in 1922 called *Rovering To Success* which warned young men to be prepared for a 'rutting stage' in their life which if not dealt with could lead to 'the habit of immorality with women or self-abuse with himself'. Readers were advised to 'keep the organ clean and bathe it in cold water' to fend off the fearsome rutting sensations.

Victorian naturalist and surgeon Frank Buckland was the founder member of a society that claimed all the animals in the world were edible for man. Buckland and his followers regularly dined on such delights as rhinoceros pie, roast ostrich, broiled porpoise head and boiled elephant's trunk. His most famous meal, however, was human. He consumed the heart of Louis XIV stolen from the monarch's tomb.

When William Strachey returned to England after living in India for the early part of his life he decided that the only accurate time in the world was in Calcutta. Consequently he lived the rest of his life in the Calcutta time zone, six hours ahead of Greenwich Mean Time. For the last fifty-six years of his life he got up in the middle of the night and was asleep by teatime.

Charles Waterton was a Victorian taxidermist who enjoyed creating monster animals from different parts of creatures he had killed. A devout Roman Catholic, he once climbed up to the lightning conductor on top of the Vatican and left his gloves there for a prank, incurring the displeasure of Pope Pius VII (he later brought them down at the Pope's request). He named his grotesque creations after well-know Protestant personalities.

Human hairball hairdresser George Limming of Hampshire died of a heart attack caused by his habit of eating his customers' hair. The amount he consumed caused his stomach to swell up, leading to the fatal attack.

George Mitchell of Hashville, Tennessee, has spent eleven of the last thirteen years in the state penitentiary because of his habit of stamping on women's toes.

Japanese staff in shops and hotels are trained to bow with an automated bowing machine called the *Ojigirenshuki*. Metal

'So what'll it be today, Sir? Just a nibble?'

plates are locked on to the body and the machine then manipulates the body to different angles. Fifteen degrees is for welcoming a colleague or customer in an entrance way, thirty degrees for greeting a customer to be served and forty-five degrees for a departing customer.

12
MOTORING MADNESS

Britain's first white line markings in the centre of the road were instigated on dangerous bends on the London to Folkestone road in Ashford, Kent in 1914. They were the idea of a farmer who was a non-motorist.

Hitler's autobahns were built in long straight stretches but experts concluded that this could induce sleep in long drives when the idea was brought to the UK. Because of this all UK motorways have been built with gentle curves.

Ray Tse, who was killed in a car crash in 1980, has a seventeen-foot gravestone, a replica of a Mercedes Benz 240-D with the dead man's name on the front number plate. Keen motorist Archie Arnold is buried in Fort Wayne, Texas, in a grave flanked by two parking meters carrying the message 'expired'.

Taxi driver George Smith achieved everlasting fame on 10 September 1897 when he became the first motorist in the UK to be convicted of drunken driving.

The Stift Phaeton car that Archduke Franz Ferdinand was travelling in when assassinated in 1914, initiating World War I, was later owned by fifteen different drivers and was involved in six major accidents that killed thirteen people. It was retired from private use in 1926 and now resides in Vienna's museum of war history.

Lada cars are known in their native country of Russia as *zhigulis*. The term Lada is used abroad for its simplicity and is derived from the Russian folk word meaning 'beloved' or 'dear one'. Zhiguli is not used abroad as the manufacturers claim it is too close to 'gigolo' in English and French and 'fake' or 'ignoramus' in Arabic.

In the United States in 1895 there were just four cars in existence. During a fair in St Louis, Missouri two of them managed to crash into each other.

In 1969 Beatrice Park drove into the River Wey at Guildford on her fifth driving test attempt. After being rescued from the roof of the vehicle the examiner was taken away in a state of shock. Undeterred, Mrs Park contacted the test centre to find out if she had passed only to be told that they could not confirm anything until the examiner submitted his report.

Soya meat was invented by Robert Boyer, a technician working at the Ford plant in Detroit in the 1930s. He discovered a way of making TVP (textured vegetable protein) whilst trying to find a substitute for leather upholstery in cars.

US drivers kill more game animals than US hunting sportsmen.

The UK's first traffic lights were installed in Parliament

'C'mon Chuck, ya can't miss!'

Square in 1868, run by gas power and hand-operated by policemen. They were discontinued shortly after when they exploded whilst in use, injuring a police constable. They did not reappear again until 1926 when an electric system was installed at Piccadilly Circus.

In the early days of US motoring a common penalty in many states for drivers who accidentally killed pedestrians was to spend an hour in a morgue with the corpse.

Sir Leslie Hore-Belisha is enshrined in British motoring legend as the transport minister who instigated pedestrian crossings in the UK complete with their flashing 'belisha beacons'. However, one of his motoring ideas was never taken up. He planned to stop speeding drivers by arming traffic cops with gongs which they would bang ferociously at offending drivers.

Percy Shaw found fame as the inventor of cat's eyes in the road and became a multi-millionaire as a result. It is a well-known fact that the idea came to him when he illuminated a real live cat's eyes in the beam of his headlights but what inspired his invention was his nightly drive to his local pub. The hostelry was situated on a particularly hazardous road full of bends and needed to be negotiated in pitch blackness. Shaw was determined to come up with a safer method of arriving home. When his cat's eye business really took off he expanded the factory in the grounds of his home and built it around a sycamore tree which he had climbed as a child.

The UK's first motorway was the Preston bypass opened

in December 1958 by the then Prime Minister Harold Macmillan. It was closed just six weeks later when a heavy frost made the surface uneven.

The world's first multi-storey car park, opened in 1901, was not in the US but in Denman Street in the heart of London. The idea was not taken up in the US until 1928.

The first traffic wardens in the UK hit the London streets on 19 September 1960. Warden Frank Shaw had the honour of administering the first ticket to a Ford Popular parked outside a hotel and belonging to a Dr Thomas Creighton who was attending a patient suffering from a heart attack. The public and press outcry at this ticketing was so great the £2 fine was waived.

In 1992 Jaguar claimed the land speed road car record of 217 mph for its XJ 220 model. That car, however, could easily be outraced by the bird, the spine-tail swift which has recorded speeds of 220 mph.

Princess Anne drives a car that has a number plate originally used on a milk float in Ealing.

Former English National Ballet dancer Gary Lambert is helping police to combat car crime in Newcastle Upon Tyne with modern dance. Young offenders aged between eleven and seventeen perform 'alternative ballet' based on breaking into cars and joy riding. The dance routine is performed against a background of sound effects which include breaking glass, revving engines and tyre screeching. Sponsored by Dance In Action the Arts Council provided the £200,000 grant to start the project.

In 1925 there were 24,564,574 cars in the world of which 21,094,980 could be found in the US.

Mrs Helen Ireland of Auburn, California, failed her driving test within a second of beginning it in the 1970s. Mistaking the accelerator for clutch she succeeded in driving straight into the wall of the test centre.

When John DeLorean's doomed car manufacturing plant in Northern Ireland went into receivership the dies to make the car bodies were sold by a scrap dealer to a fish farmer in Cork. The twelve five-ton sections were used to pin down fishing nets. Their original cost when built for manufacturing purposes was over $10 million.

Evangelical churchgoers have been warned not to drive their cars by the police if they have received the 'Toronto blessing'. The blessing delivered during services has seen churchgoers claiming they have become possessed by the Holy Spirit. Recipients fall over and laugh hysterically giving the image of drunkenness. Dr Patrick Dixon, a Christian doctor, has warned the effects could lead to accidents. Over 4,000 churchgoers in Great Britain have experienced the sensation and many are now being carried to their car after services.

In 1930 Charles Creighton and James Hargis drove

How not to start your driving test.

a Model A Ford from New York to Los Angeles in reverse without stopping the engine, turned around and reversed all the way back.

Egypt's driving test of steering a car forwards and backwards a distance of six feet has now been made harder by painting white lines at the appointed stopping marks.

When postman Graham Evans caused a major accident, crashing his red Astra van into an Escort and a Rover and running up a bill for damage of thousands of pounds, he had a unique excuse for the magistrates' court. He claimed that his distinctly untrendy blue nylon postie trousers caused him to lose control of the vehicle. He told the court, 'They were rubbing into my groin. I felt great discomfort, the pain was intense.' The magistrate did not accept his argument however and he was fined £180. Royal mail chiefs were more sympathetic and allowed him to keep his job. The red-faced postman told reporters, 'Let's face it, it's not something I'd have made up. It's very embarrassing. I'm well known in the area and I'm going to get a lot of stick.'

In parts of the United Arab Emirates camels wear fluorescent jackets so they can be spotted easily by motorists.

Britain's speed limit for mechanically driven vehicles in 1864 was just 2 mph.

Traffic Court was a popular programme on US TV in 1958. Actors were used to recreate thrilling courtroom dramas over subjects such as parking in a no-parking zone, exceeding the speed limit or just failing to signal.

In the 1950s an Argentinian criminal gang dismantled an iron road bridge crossing Rio Parana overnight and sold it to local scrap merchants.

13

ONLY IN THE UNITED STATES OF AMERICA

Louisville radio station WDXJ launched a competition for listeners to produce the most creative depiction of the station's name. Twenty-year-old Elaine Houghland submitted a display of dead animals (including cats and chickens) wired to a board in the shape of the letters WDXJ. Houghland claimed she had found the animals dead in the road but a local animal agency claimed she had killed them to win the contest.

Construction supplier Sam Krogstad posted an entire harbour through the US mail system in 1988. Broken up into concrete blocks it was sent from Anchorage, Alaska 700 miles north to Wainwright. Krogstad was quite within his rights to use the postie and save himself thousands of dollars in what he would have paid in shipping fees.

A prisoner at Massachusetts' Deer Island prison refused to climb down from the jail roof unless prison warders and officials could name all six children from *The Brady Bunch*. No one on the staff could come up with the answer, but the prisoner surrendered after five hours.

Crazy Mike's chain of video stores in Seattle offers free video rentals for a year to anyone in exchange for guns. So far they have collected almost 300 weapons.

Daimion Osby of Fort Worth, Texas, admitted to killing two unarmed men who had harassed him over a gambling win but his defence in court was that he was reacting under the influence of 'urban survival syndrome'. His lawyer claimed this was a 'fear that black people have of other black people' in an urban situation. The court was told that Osby used his gun like an American Express card and never left home without it.

US president Harry Truman was convinced that no one paid any attention to him when he was introduced at White House receptions as they were so overawed by his presence. He tested his theory out on one occasion by greeting all his guests with the phrase, 'I killed my grandmother this morning'. No one questioned his statement merely smiling and thanking him. One guest however was wise to his plan and replied, 'She had it coming.'

The gas chamber was introduced in some US states in 1924 to give what was claimed a more humane style of execution after misfunctions with the electric chair. The chamber was used after the original plan to release gas into the cell of unsuspecting condemned men was proved impractical. Gee Jon was the first criminal executed in such a chamber on 8 February 1924.

In the state of Texas in 1990 more people were killed by guns (3,443) than in traffic accidents (3,309).

US jockey Ralph Neves was pronounced dead after a fall

at the Bay Meadows racetrack in 1936 by three different doctors. After a minute's silence from the spectators his body was removed to a morgue in the nearest town. He revived, however, shortly after and wearing only a hospital gown took a taxi back to the course where he alarmed the crowd with his miraculous reappearance. Neves rode again on the next day's racing card.

Members of the Eskimo community of Little Diomede, Alaska, are the only US citizens who do not pay income tax. Instead of money they are allowed to pay with seal tusks.

The National Tattoo Association Of America estimate that one in ten Americans has a tattoo of some kind.

Sherman Cohen, the programme director of Radio KHYT of Tucson, Arizona, gives astrological readings based on songs that were number one when a subject was born. Throughout the years he claims that the number one on the day you were born has the most influence on your future life. When Michael Jackson was born on 29 August 1958 the US number one was Little Star by the Elegants. Mariah Carey, born on 22 March 1970, was named by her mother after her favourite song from the musical *Paint Your Wagon*. That tune was 'They Call the Wind Mariah'. Lee Marvin's number one from the same show, 'Wanderin' Star', was number one in the UK that very week.

Montpelier, Vermont plays host every year to the American Rotten Sneakers Contest.

A group of irate women passengers decided to travel topless

on New York's subway system in protest against transport regulations that allowed men to travel shirtless but not women. They armed themselves with water pistols to protect themselves against voyeurs. The authorities were so impressed with their stand they altered the rules to allow them to travel that way to if they so desired.

Carl Stevens of Knoxville, Illinois, was nursed for eight years for a serious illness by his wife and two children until it was revealed to them that he had been dead for this entire period. Town sheriff Mark Shearer told the press, 'Let's just say the family has abnormal beliefs in the power of healing.'

In 1940 a proposal was made to build a 300-foot statue on the summit of Mount Battle, Maine in honour of the inventor of the doughnut hole, Captain Hansen Gregory. It was to be lit by floodlights so it could be seen fifty miles out to sea. The money was never raised to build this eighth wonder of the world.

In 1985 the Fairmount Hotel in San Antonio, Texas, was transported four blocks from the site where it was originally built in 1906. Weighing 3.2 million pounds it was moved to make way for a shopping mall.

The National Foundation for the Chemically Sensitive in Marin County, California, is campaigning to ban the use of perfume in public places. They refer to it as 'discretionary fragrance' and claim it is politically incorrect to wear perfume or cologne in the presence of others as they may be allergic to it.

A US study in 1984 showed that 8,000 Americans a year suffer injury in toothpick-related incidents. Commonest accidents are swallowing the pick or puncturing the eye or the ear. Many of the accidents are fatal.

In Indiana it is illegal to travel on a bus within four hours of eating garlic.

Dallas DJ Ron Chapman told listeners to his show that if they sent him $20 he would send them nothing by return. A week later he had received over $240,000. I might try that myself!

US department stores used a subliminal message system in the 1970s mixed in with their diet of muzak which contained such phrases as 'I am honest and I will not steal'. They reported a major decrease in shoplifting.

Top 1950s US TV chat show host Steve Allen was a keen boogie woogie piano player but achieved hardly any sales when he released records. When he posed as black blues man Buck Hammer his sales soared. He employed his black housekeeper Mary Sears to appear on the cover of his release *The Wild Piano of Mary Ann Jackson* and once again scored a hit with blues and jazz fans.

In Waterloo, Nebraska, it is illegal for barbers to eat onions between 7 a.m. and 7 p.m.

Americans spend an estimated $10 billion dollars a

year on recorded music but the porn industry claims an estimated $12 billion take.

At Long Beach, California, in December 1976 a dummy hanging in an amusement park was discovered to be a real life corpse. The decaying body had hung for five years at the same spot. When an episode of TV's *The Six Million Dollar Man* was being filmed at the park a technician noticed a bone protruding and alerted the authorities. The five foot three inch cadaver weighed in at 159 lbs and was wrapped in gauze sprayed in fluorescent paint. It had been bought from a local wax museum.

In New York in 1977 Mrs Ellen Cooperman was allowed to change her name to Ellen Cooperperson on the grounds the old name was sexist after divorcing film producer Norman Cooperman.

In the second half of the twentieth century oral sex was still forbidden by law in most US states, even between husband and wife in Kentucky and South Carolina where it was rated a felony. In New York it was classified as a misdemeanour. In Illinois, Wisconsin, Missouri and Ohio oral sex was permitted if performed by a man but illegal if committed by a woman.

Dr Richard Willard of Chicago University set out in 1977 to increase the breast size of women by the use of hypnotism. He fed his subjects images of large rounded breasts with erect nipples. His report in the *American Journal of Clinical Hypnosis* claimed that 46 per cent had increased their bra size.

In Minnesota it is illegal to hang male and female clothing together on a washing line.

New Jersey housewife Mary Kuhery left her husband two dollars in her will which he inherited only on the condition that he spent half of it on a rope to hang himself with.

In the USA any ransom money paid to kidnappers is tax deductible.

The University of California has discovered that hamburger and other fast food restaurants create more pollution in Los Angles than the city's buses. They release an estimated 13.7 tons of smoke and 19 tons of organic compounds into the atmosphere each day. They could be contributing greatly to cancer and respiratory problems amongst the city's vast population. The main problem is perceived to be that most of the 30,000 restaurants in Los Angeles use charcoal grills where fat drops on to naked flames and burns at high temperature, creating the dangerous smog.

Before President Richard Nixon made his historic trip to China in the 1970s members of his advance team ordered that any toilet seat coming into contact with the Presidential posterior had to be made of plastic. They had discovered that many Chinese seats were made from the wood of the poisonous sumal plant which created vicious skin disorders on western bottoms.

Nathaniel Bordanove, a Republican candidate for the

'Forget Fifth Avenue – head straight for GO!'

mayorship of Warwick, New Jersey, managed to be elected eight days after his death.

The US Customs Service regularly confiscates planes used by drug smugglers and sells them at auction for prices way below their market value. The biggest customers for these aviation bargains are drug smugglers.

Americans hold the record for underwater Monopoly playing. The Buffalo Drive Club, comprising 350 members, played non-stop for 1,080 hours in 1983, a total of 45 days.

Chicago neurologist and psychiatrist Dr Alan Hirsch revealed at a recent seminar the smells that really turn men on. He measured the power of different pongs by analysing the increase in blood flow amongst a team of volunteers when exposed to different whiffs. Pumpkin pie and lavender triggered the most powerful response with a 40 per cent increase whilst lavender and black licorice scored second with 32 per cent and 20 per cent fell for doughnuts and pumpkin pie. Men who had sex frequently enjoyed the smell of Coca-Cola, lavender and oriental spices while older men plumped for vanilla. Hirsch plans to open a clinic for impotent men who will be treated to respond to smells which could remind them of their youth. Hirsch explains, 'It could be a conditioned Pavlovian response reminding men of their girlfriends or wives or it could be that the smell triggers a vivid memory of the past to put them in a positive mood.'

In Los Angeles, California, in March 1961 Douglas Johnston discovered $100,000 in the street which he

'Now, Eunice, I *warned* you not to choose vanilla
with Uncle Bert around!'

promptly handed in to his local police station. When his honesty was publicised in the press he received thousands of letters not from well wishers but from people telling him he must be insane.

In the 1950s research was conducted at the National Marine Laboratory in Maryland into the effects of creating a wave motion in a goldfish bowl and the reactions of the fish. After years of study it was decided that goldfish probably became seasick.

Over twice as many Americans died by gunshot wounds in the US during the period of the Vietnam War than died fighting in Vietnam.

The North American Bait Company organised a Cooking with Worms competition in 1986. The winner was Earth-worm Applesauce Surprise Cake.

In 1929 Otto E. Funk walked from New York to San Francisco playing the violin for the whole journey.

In 1977 the Warrenton Fauquier newspaper of Virginia published the *Easy Sky Diving Book*. However they had to quickly publish a correction which stated 'On page eight, line seven the words "state zip code" should read – "pull rip cord".'

14

PARTS OF
THE BODY

Underwear manufacturers Jockey have spent £50,000 on intensive research which proves that since the 1930s they have misjudged the male torso. It has always been assumed that the measurement from groin to navel varied in proportion to a man's waist, a widely-held belief of tailors. Jockey's research now reveals that the distance is almost always constant varying by only two per cent regardless of waistline. Their new design in men's underpants is therefore lower around the stomach and more supportive and snug.

The Men's Institute of Cosmetic Surgery claims to be the largest organisation in the world dedicated to penis enlargement. Surgeons use a method that removes three inches of penis root from behind the pelvic bone and places it in front with added fat deposits to give the organ a larger circumference.

Sneezes leave the human body at 85 per cent of the speed of sound.

Body odour emanates from the apocrine glands which develop during puberty and are found on the face, chest, armpits, genitals and anus. These odours are often used as signs of friendship in many races. Some tribes in New Guinea say goodbye by cupping each others armpit and then stroking their body.

Lovers in Elizabethan times would exchange 'love apples' when plighting their troth. Peeled apples were kept under respective armpits until saturated with sweat and then inhaled by male and female as a reminder of their love.

The medical reference book *The Merck Manual* devotes a chapter to functional bowel disease, a scholarly study of farting. It concludes that tests on an average patient produced 141 farts on a daily basis with 70 occurring in a 4-hour period. The manual breaks down anal emissions into three forms. Firstly 'The Slider' which is released noiselessly, sometimes with devastating effect. Secondly 'The Open Sphincter' or 'Pooh' type which is said to be of higher temperature and more aromatic and thirdly 'The Staccato' or 'Drum Beat' type, pleasantly passed in privacy.

The art of tattooing in Japan is known as irezumi and is performed by tattoo masters who sometimes create full body tattoos. Classic examples of the art are often donated by clients after their death to be framed and displayed at Tokyo University.

A prick of the skin sends a signal of pain to the brain at 98 feet per second. Burns or aches register more slowly at 6 feet per second whilst some leg pain registers at 425 feet per second.

The 'Sourtoe Cocktail' was invented at the Eldorado

Hotel in Dawson City in the Yukonin in 1973. It involved placing a human toe in an alcoholic drink and reciting the rhyme, 'You can drink it fast you can drink it slow but the lips have gotta touch the toe.' When a miner accidentally consumed the toe it was replaced by a toe amputee from Alberta, Canada.

Frank Lentini was known as the 'King of the Freaks' as he toured America in the late nineteenth century. He displayed an extra set of genitals, four feet, sixteen toes and three legs, one of which grew out of the base of his spine that he used as a stool. In his circus act he used the extra limb to kick a football the length of the big top.

Professor Albert Einstein's brain was preserved after his death to enable scientists to analyse what made the great man a genius. Little information was forthcoming as it was cut up in slivers and sent to specialists across the US by a Dr Harvey at Princeton University. The remains of the brain were discovered in the 1970s inside an old cider carton in doctor Harvey's office.

Nineteen-year-old South African Kallie Fortuin was forced to castrate himself at gunpoint after raping an old woman and being apprehended by her son and a friend. He astonished medical staff when admitted to hospital at the perfection of his non-surgical removal of his penis. Fortuin explained he had seen the operation performed on pigs and applied this experience under threat. He escaped the death sentence because of his ordeal and was ordered to serve ten years.

Archaeologists often determine the age of Greek and

'Aw, hell Joe! *Touch* the toe, we said, not
swallow the dang thing!'

Roman statues of naked males by the size of their testicles.

Mrs Jack Crackers wrote to the *Bradford Argus* in 1987 about her husband's deafness. She claimed he had been deaf for most of his seventy-five years but whilst on holiday in Sweden he had been saved from choking by a strong thump on the back. A bus ticket issued in Buxton, Derbyshire almost sixty-five years before emerged from his ear and his hearing was restored. Mr Crackers said later that he thought he may have placed the ticket in his ear whilst on his way home from school as a child.

In 1939 Japanese prime minister Fumimaro Konoye refused to travel to an important cabinet meeting with Foreign Minister Yosuke Matsuoka because he was suffering from piles. Matsuoka had wanted to clear up a misunderstanding with Konoye about US peace proposals. Many political commentators felt that if the meeting had taken place Japan may not have embarked into war with the US.

Accounts of nineteenth-century murders in the UK held in public record offices are often bound in the skin of the accused. Bristol's office contains the transcript of the murder trial in 1821 of John Horwood for the murder of a girl called Eliza Balsam. The volume is covered by Horwood's skin and contains an account of the dissection by surgeon Richard Smith.

The Journal of the American Medical Association reported

the case of a patient in December 1960 who complained of swollen ankles and was found to have 258 items in his stomach. They included 16 religious medals, 3 sets of rosary beads, a 3 lb piece of metal, 26 keys, a bracelet, a necklace, 3 pairs of tweezers, 4 nail clippers, 39 nail files, 3 metal chains and 88 assorted coins.

Jose Luis Astoreka won the world's first competition for cracking walnuts in the anus in the Basque village of Kortezubi, Spain, in 1990. He demolished thirty walnuts between his cheeks in just fifty-seven seconds. His brother achieved second place with eighty seconds.

Modern Manners – The Essential Guide to Living in the 90s by Drusilla Beyfus can only offer the following advice to anyone who feels they are about to blow off in public. 'If a person suspects they are going to fart, their best move is to try and step away from the group.'

Napoleon's penis appeared as a sale item at Christie's auctioneers in 1972. The shrunken one-inch long member was described as having the appearance of a 'sea horse' and failed to reach its reserve price in the sale.

Terrorists in the Phillipines in 1987 were found to be using human kneecaps around their necks as a crude form of body armour.

The average human body has enough phosphorus to make 2,000 matches, 20 square feet of skin, enough iron to make a nail, enough potassium to explode a small cannon and enough carbon to produce the lead for 9,000 pencils.

Painter Toulouse-Lautrec suffered from restricted growth because he broke both legs as a young man. He also suffered from hypertrophy, exaggerated growth of the penis.

Lady Coventry died in 1760 through the effects of continually painting her face with white lead.

In her old age Queen Elizabeth I stuffed her mouth with cloth in order to compensate for the effect of her sunken cheeks.

Frank Bruno, Wincey Willis, Dave Lee Travis, Cliff Richard, Mike Yarwood and David Dimbleby all have something in common. They have all at one time been voted Heads of the year by the National Hairdresser's Federation.

The tubes inside a man's testicles which carry sperm to the penis are more than twenty feet long. Over 177,181,200 billion sperm are ejected in England and Wales each year.

The most popular form of plastic surgery in the US is not facelifts or breast enlargement. Liposuction or 'fat sucking' is the clear winner with over 100,000 operations per year.

A medical textbook offers the following handy hints for those going about the removal of items from the back passage. 'The variety of foreign bodies which have found their way into the rectum is hardly less remarkable than the ingenuity displayed in their removal. A turnip has been delivered *per anum* by the use of obstetric forceps.

A stick firmly impacted has been withdrawn by inserting a gimlet into its lower end. A tumbler mouth looking downwards has several times been extracted by filling the interior with a wet plaster of paris bandage, leaving the end of the bandage extruding and allowing the plaster to set.'

A Dr Russell of Edinburgh published his *Observations on Testicles* in 1833. He claimed to have found a scrotum with no less than six testicles and also a monk with three who was unable to keep his vow of chastity.

15
ROCK AND POP

After Mariah Carey found her enormous fame as one of the biggest pop stars in the world her stepfather Joseph Vian took her to court seeking compensation for the financial and emotional support he gave her before she had a hit. He claimed she had promised to repay him when successful for his purchase of an apartment, a car and the dazzling dental work which undoubtedly sped her on the ladder of success. He also claimed Mariah had actively sought to break up the relationship between himself and her natural mother when Patricia Carey filed for divorce.

In 1989 Jon Bon Jovi and his future wife Dorothea Hurley were both charged with trespass in New York. Their crime? Skating on a public ice rink at 3.30 a.m.

When the earliest version of the Beatles, the Quarry Men, made their debut at Liverpool's famous Cavern Club in August 1957, Paul McCartney did not make an appearance because of a pressing engagement. He was away at scout camp.

Charles Gates Dawes is the only known former Vice-President of the United States to pen a US chart topping hit. In 1912 he wrote a tune called 'Melody in A Major' which was given lyrics by songwriter Carl Sigman in 1951 and turned it into 'It's All in the Game', which Tommy Edwards took to number one for six weeks in 1958. Dawes served as Vice-President under Calvin Coolidge from 1925 to 1929.

A recording session by Elvis Presley in April 1956 held in Nashville, the country capital, produced only one song after the singer's plane was forced to make an emergency landing en route to the studio when one of the engines cut out. A nervous Elvis cut only one song, 'I Want You, I Need You, I Love You' which later topped the US chart. On one take of the song he mistakenly sang 'I Need You, I Want You, I Love You'.

Jahn Ivar 'Mini' Jakobsen faced a double blow after Norway were knocked out of the 1994 World Cup in the first round. The Norwegian international was a big fan of musician and fellow countryman Jahn Teigen who achieved notoriety after receiving 'nil points' during the 1978 Eurovision Song Contest. He even changed his christian name from Jan to Jahn in honour of the singer. Teigen had promised to write a song about his friend if he scored in the competition but these hopes were wrecked when the Republic of Ireland bumped them out of the championships with a nil-nil draw.

My son Tommy's favourite soul classic 'When a Man Loves a Woman' was written for Percy Sledge by two members of his backing band, Cameron Lewis and Arthur Wright. They wrote it on the spot after Sledge told them he was too upset over a broken love affair to perform his usual set of cover versions.

Former Monkees star Mike Nesmith is a wealthy man outside of his main projects of music and film. His mother invented typist's correction fluid. In the 1950s Bette Nesmith Graham was a hopeless typist and to avoid the sack in her job she used tempera waterbase paint to cover up her errors. She refined the process with the help of Mike's chemistry teacher and named her invention 'liquid paper'. She launched a cottage industry with the help of her schoolboy son who collected old bottles to contain the product which later became an essential in every office.

A military coup in Portugal was signalled to begin by the broadcast of a Portugese Eurovision Song Contest entry on the radio.

Barry McGuire's dirge, 'Eve of Destruction', is probably one of the most famous protest songs of the 1960s but the record that was released was just a rough vocal track which was rushed into shops. McGuire intended to deliver a more polished product but because the demo was released to a DJ who played it immediately on his show, public demand proved too much and it was released in its original form and was a worldwide hit.

Bachman Turner Overdrive originally recorded 'You Ain't Seen Nothing Yet' as a private joke against their manager Gary Bachman, brother of group leader Randy Bachman, who was a compulsive stutterer. The in joke was heard by a record company executive who insisted they release it. The group attempted to record it without the stutter but reverted to the original which became a massive hit.

The Million Dollar Quartet is the name given to a legendary recording made at the Sun studios in 1956 when Elvis Presley, Jerry Lee Lewis, Carl Perkins and Johnny Cash met to sing some of their favourite songs. Cash was photographed as part of the epoch-making line up but did not sing on the session. He decided to go Christmas shopping with his wife instead.

Roberta Flack's 'Killing Me Softly with His Song' was written in response to Don McLean's performance of 'American Pie' at a Los Angeles concert.

Phil Spector's first major hit with the Teddy Bears, 'To Know Him is to Love Him' was based on the epitaph on his father's grave: 'To Know Him Was to Love Him.'

Frank Zappa named his four children Moon Unit, Dweezil, Ahmet Rodin and Diva.

Ernie K Doe's 'Mother-In-Law', a humorous tale of the perils of marriage, was rescued from a rubbish bin by Doe at songwriter Allen Toussaint's house. Doe's own marriage suffered from mother-in-law problems and he insisted on recording the song. It went on to top the charts in 1961.

'Happy Birthday' is the most widely sung song in the world but it was only published in 1935. Originally written by sisters Mildred and Patty Hill as 'Good Morning to You' the words were altered and the title is still a registered copyright. The writers still receive a royalty for its use in any film.

Culture Club were named because of the diverse nationalities of its members. Vocalist Boy George was of Irish origin, bassist Mikey Craig Jamaican, drummer Jon Moss Jewish and guitarist Roy Hay English.

Guy Mitchell's 1950 US hit 'My Heart Cries' was supposedly based on a song written by former French queen Marie Antoinette who was beheaded in the French Revolution.

Elvis Presley appeared in a TV commercial for 'Southern Made' doughnuts in 1954.

Queen had their first hit, 'Seven Seas of Rhye' in 1974 and went on to success throughout the world, becoming one of the all-time greatest bands in pop history. Members Freddie Mercury, Brian May, John Deacon and Roger Taylor hold a distinction which remains unique in pop history. Each member has individually penned a top ten hit.

Elvis Presley's rock 'n' roll classic 'Heartbreak Hotel' was written by Mae Boren Axton, Tommy Durden and Elvis and was based on a newspaper story where a suicide victim left a one line note, 'I walk a lonely street.'

Fifteen-year-old Paul Anka's chart topper 'Diana' was

originally written by Anka as a poem of devotion to the babysitter of his younger brother and sister who was three years older than him.

Brian Hyland's hit 'Itsy Bitsy Teenie Weenie Yellow Polka Dot Bikini' was penned by songwriter Paul Vance whilst watching his two-year-old daughter playing on a beach in said apparel.

Barbra Streisand and Neil Diamond both recorded 'You Don't Bring Me Flowers' separately on their respective 1978 albums before Kentucky DJ Gary Clark spliced both their vocals together to create a duet. It proved so popular that the singing superstars felt obliged to join together in a studio and sing it for real and it went on to top the US chart. Clark later attempted to sue record company CBS for $5 million dollars as he had not been rewarded for his idea.

Buddy Holly hired a charter plane to transport him between concerts on his Winter Party Dance Tour of 1959 as he became increasingly fed up with travelling in a tour bus with minimal heating. He was also keen to catch up with his laundry. He died when the plane crashed on 3 February 1959 along with the Big Bopper and Ritchie Valens. Holly's original passengers were set to be future country legend Waylon Jennings, who gave up his seat to the Big Bopper, and Tommy Allsup who gave up his seat on the toss of a coin to Ritchie Valens.

Elvis Presley's former home Graceland has now become

one of the most visited houses in America but it was not named by the singing star. It was built by Dr Thomas Moore who named it in honour of his Aunt Grace. Elvis bought the property for $100,000.

Daryl Hall and John Oates first met each other in a lift at Philadelphia's Adelphi Ballroom whilst hiding from a vicious gang fight.

Acker Bilk learnt to play the clarinet because he fell asleep on guard duty whilst serving with the army in Egypt shortly after World War II. Imprisoned for three months he took up the instrument to pass the time. Born Bernard Stanley Bilk he added Acker, slang for mate, when he entered showbiz.

Herb Alpert's 1979 hit 'Rise', a slow-paced instrumental, became a big dance hit in the UK in 1979. Imported 12-inch copies from the US played at 33 ⅓ rpm but British DJs mistakenly played the disc at 45 rpm, creating an up-tempo hit.

Robert Van Winkle found fame in 1990 as Vanilla Ice. His debut album sold an astonishing seven million copies worldwide.

On 8 December 1961 small-time pop quartet the Beatles headed south for a nine-hour journey on their first ever trip to play in the south of England. With their first hit still a year away the group were unknown outside of their native Liverpool so the omens for a large turnout at the Palais Ballroom, Aldershot, were not good. Due to an advertising blunder the hall remained resolutely empty until the panicking promoter managed to round up eighteen hardy souls from local pubs and clubs who coughed up 5/- (25p) each to witness the beat session. In the 1980s Paul McCartney reminisced about the night as 'the time we couldn't get arrested', referring to the fact that the local constabulary were waiting outside the dance hall at the conclusion of their set ordering them to leave Aldershot and never return.

Drugs, groupies, the destruction of hotel rooms and rock 'n' roll excess in general are commonplace in this day and age but it is a little known fact that the Beatles were the originators of bad behaviour as far back as 1962. After appearing on the bottom of a six-act bill at the ABC Cinema, Carlisle, the soon-to-be-fab foursome decided on a wild night out on the town with fellow tour acts Helen Shapiro and Kenny Lynch. Their chosen venue to groove the night away was the Crown and Mitre Hotel where they gatecrashed the Carlisle Golf Club Dance. They were immediately escorted from the premises after upsetting members by appearing in the ballroom wearing leather jackets.

The banjo is the only musical instrument to have originated in the US.

After Norway's disastrous run of three single-point scores in the Eurovision Song Contest a professor of linguistics was hired to smooth out unpleasant Scandinavian sounds in the songs.

16
SEX

In many English towns and cities signs of mediaeval prostitution still remain with street names such as Maiden Lane or Love Lane. In the City of London Gropecunt Street and Codpiece Alley have been renamed Grape Street and Coppice Alley. Streets that have disappeared in the City completely include Whore's Nest, Cuckold Court and Slut's Hole.

Virgin prostitutes were most sought-after by amorous Victorians and many faked their virginity by placing bags of pigeon blood in their vaginas.

Transsexual immigrants are flooding Germany as red-blooded teutons continue to marry what they think are pretty Thai girls. The husbands are fooled by extensive plastic surgery which deceives them even in the marital bed. Police report that many of the 'girls' work as hookers and have become involved in vicious street fights with customers. Some are so aggressive they carry tear gas, knives and shotguns and are adept at martial arts.

Oral stimulation of the anus can politely be referred to as 'feuille de rose'.

Carlos Cesaro of Lima, Peru, had to hit his wife about the head with an alarm clock when she suffered an epileptic fit whilst performing oral sex on him. Cesaro received nine stitches in his penis and his wife vowed not to perform oral sex with him again.

The Los Angeles Hung Jury Club has a 2,000-strong membership of men who can boast penises longer than eight inches. Apart from a social society the club also acts as a dating agency for women who like well hung men.

Postillionage involves placing your finger in a loved one's anus before orgasm.

An exhibition of photographs of naked men by British photographer Ajamu at the Metropolitan Gallery, Manchester, was censored after a flood of complaints even before it opened. The pictures, featuring men with erections, had created no controversy when shown in London but Manchester decided to cover up the offending genitals with sheets of white paper. Mrs Alison Radovanovic from the gallery explained, 'I decided to act after checking the law: it seems that the pictures are illegal because of the angle of the erections. It is a shame because the pictures are important as works of art.' A spokesman for the Vice Squad said, 'You can show pictures of naked men without erections but it is illegal to show naked men with erection.' The exhibition was part of a festival entitled 'It's Queer Up North'.

The phrase hanky panky stems from leading Victorian erotica collector Frederick Hanky whose massive repository of filth included much of the Marquis De Sade's memorabilia.

The Japanese used a wide range of sex aids long before their manufacture became a major money spinning industry. Men used a 'yoroi-gata', a latticed shaft-like tube to increase their manhood or strapped on a 'higozuiki', a set of thongs which boosted the power of their erection. Women were also keen on the 'engia', a dildo that strapped to the heel while the ankle was held up by a support around the neck.

Silent film star Clara Bow was alleged in the 1920s to have had sex with the entire University of Southern California football team in one steamy session. The team were known as the 'Thundering Herd' and Miss Bow even managed to accommodate the eleventh man, Marion Morrison, who later went on to fame as John Wayne.

Penis captivus is the comparatively rare medical condition when a man's penis becomes trapped in a woman's vagina. It was well known in mediaeval times as it was claimed it affected anyone who copulated in a church or churchyard. It was seen as God's revenge on the couple. The dreaded *captivus* struck one couple in a Warsaw park in 1923 and they were so ashamed by the resulting press coverage they shot themselves.

The phrase 'red light district' derives from the habit of early American railroad men of leaving their red signal lamps outside brothels so they could instantly be located in case of emergency.

In 1978 fewer than 1 per cent of US homes had a video recorder. However 75 per cent of their use at that time was thought to be for the playing back of pornographic videos.

Johnny Carson was America's number one chat show host for over thirty years and was a master of the speedy retort. When Raquel Welch appeared on his show with a white kitten on her lap she asked him, 'Would you like to see my pussy?' He immediately fired back the zinger, 'I will if you move the damn cat.'

Masturbation emanates from the Latin word *manystuprare* which literally translated means 'to defile with the hand'.

The first test of the contraceptive pill was made on 1,300 women in a slum housing project in San Juan, Puerto Rico in the 1950s. At the the end of the three-year trial only seventeen women had become pregnant. It was also tested on some of the women's husbands but the only effect was to cause their testicles to swell up.

Durex contraceptives were launched by the London Rubber Company in 1932. The name derived from durability, reliability and excellence. The original packaging boasted that the product 'prevents nervous strain'. Although available in vending machines in pubs and clubs for years it was only in 1992 that they became available from a machine in a public place when one was located in Nuneaton bus station.

Fornication derives from the Latin word fornix which was a vaulted or arched basement found in a Roman villa used as a brothel by prostitutes.

When Tampax tampons were launched in the UK in the 1940s the revered British medical journal *The Lancet* claimed that virgins would not be able to use them without losing their virginity. This patently untrue statement perpetuated a myth that lived on until 1956 when the General Medical Council warning on all Tampax packets, 'unsuitable for unmarried women', was quietly dropped.

A photograph of Princess Diana was used on posters promoting birth control in Pakistan as a shining example to the populace because she only had two children.

The world's longest penis in the animal family is owned by the blue whale with an average length of ten feet.

The Corduroy Club in London is a haven for fetishists of the ribbed material who love its feel against their flesh. It rivals rubber and PVC, and many fetishists claim it revives sexual memories of wearing corduroy shorts in their youth. Some members claim to be stimulated by the aroma of tinned peaches emanating from a chemical used in their manufacture.

In terms of smutty postcards Great Britain led the world in the first half of the century. The biggest selling postcard in this country was designed by comic artist Donald McGill. It featured a man asking a woman, 'How do you like Kipling?' to which she replies, 'I don't know, you naughty boy, I've never kippled.'

There are an estimated six million eunuchs in the world with over 20 per cent of them to be found in India.

In ancient Egypt goats were used to determine if a woman

Ribbed Rapture.

was a lesbian. The accused would be approached by the court goat. If it showed interest in her she would be found innocent but if it ignored her she would be found guilty.

Any men planning on taking a Club 18–30 holiday should heed the treatment detailed in the US Medical Annual for 1913 on the treatment of sexual diseases. 'In those who have been exposed to infection the entire penis is scrubbed with liquid soap and water for several minutes and then washed with mercuric perchloride lotion 1:2,000. Abrasions are sprayed with hydrogen peroxide. Two urethral injections of argyrol (10 per cent) are then given and retained for five minutes. The whole penis is then rubbed with 33 per cent calomel ointment which is kept on for several hours.'

The placing of cards by prostitutes advertising their wares in telephone boxes in London is regarded as a contemporary problem but Edwardians faced similar blatant promotion of services on offer. Modern times have given us phrases such as 'TV and large chest for sale' but all men in the know at the beginning of the century would be aware of the implications of 'French lessons given by a French mistress' which littered the classified columns of newspapers. Edwardians also had their own massage parlours which advertised the virtues of nurses offering a wide range of 'special oil and electrical treatments for all muscular ailments'. Sandwich board men were regularly employed to walk the streets of Piccadilly Circus extolling the services of these establishments.

Men engaging in sexual relations with vacuum cleaner hoses are mainly confined to the fifty-five to sixty-five age group, a recent survey shows. In an exhaustive survey across the US a wide cross-section of vacuum love has been recorded. A railway signalman was found naked in his box on the receiving end of a hose whilst another victim saved by the rescue services claimed that the pelmet cleaning attachment connected to his penis got there because he was changing the plug in the nude. The Hoover Dusterette was found to be the most hazardous (not the Goblin, surprisingly) mainly due to the close proximity of the whirring motor to the hose attachment.

Homosexuality in Great Britain was very strictly dealt with by the authorities before World War I. Any type of sexual contact between members of the same sex could result in a sentence of birching (which a few victims may have enjoyed) or a year of hard labour. Court records highlight cases of such men as a shop worker aged seventeen who was found trolling the streets in 'a golden haired wig, the long tresses of which were tied back with a long black bow'. A 29-year-old valet was exposed to a court as a 'shameless and dangerous character frequenting the West End with face rouged and powdered and eyebrows pencilled'. He received nine months' hard labour and twenty-five strokes of the birch.

Miguel Aromina was in the wrong place at the wrong time when his wife discovered proof of a longstanding affair with another woman. Wife Santana discovered a pair of women's panties in the fickle husband's jacket at their Mexico City home. As Miguel cooked spicy Mexican sausages in his underpants she attacked him with a bread knife, severing his penis with one stroke. When paramedics arrived they grabbed what they thought was the unfortunate Mexican's penis, packed it in ice and rushed him and it to the nearest hospital. As surgeons prepared to sew on the missing member a sharp eyed nurse noticed fork pricks in the prick and called a halt to the operation. The half-cooked sausage was removed immediately and paramedics rushed back to the house to find the errant penis. It was finally located beneath the cooker sticky with ancient cooking oil and chili. After a quick soak it was reunited with its owner after a six-hour operation.

The National Union of Women Workers was set up in October 1914 to protect the moral welfare of girls who might be corrupted by servicemen. Aged between thirty and fifty, its members armed themselves with ID cards and armbands and patrolled near army camps, docks and depots, on the hunt for courting couples who they would expose with their bright lanterns. Cinemas and dark alleys were their favourite hunting grounds and they were often instrumental in having public seating removed in desolate areas to discourage impolite loitering.

Prosecution for acts of indecency between men in the early decades of this century often took place in criminal courts in front of a jury in preference to a magistrate because a verdict of not guilty was almost invariably obtained. Defence lawyers discovered that it was almost impossible for the jury to reach a majority decision in most cases because average jurors simply refused to believe men could behave in such a manner to each other.

Sodomy is believed to be a cure for VD in parts of the Far East.

Roger LeFranc and girlfriend Remy Dilors little thought that within one hour of taking their seats at the Casino Cinema, Paris, on a summer's night in 1978 they would be in a casualty ward undergoing extensive surgery usually reserved for separating siamese twins. Watching a dubbed version of *Carry On Camping* proved of little interest to the gallic lovers and the comic antics of Kenneth Williams and Barbara Windsor had no charms for them. They found solace in each others' arms and were soon locked together in the near deserted cinema. However, as their passion mounted Remy's leg became firmly wedged in the tip-up cinema seat while Roger's arm became wedged between the seat-backs. As the closing credits filled the screen and the cinema emptied the couple found themselves trapped and emergency services were called. French fireman sawed away at the seats until room could be made to manoeuvre them through the exit doors. In a bustling Parisian street the cutting away operation continued on the love-locked couple until enough seating was removed to get them in an ambulance. An operation in hospital finally did the trick as their interlocked bodies were unprised using muscle relaxants and a surgical hydraulic jack.

One of the first textbooks on masturbation was published in London in the eighteenth century. It was called *Onania or the Heinous Sin of Self-Pollution and All Its Frightful Consequences*. An early sex education book recognised frequent masturbators as having 'shifty glances and wearing caps pulled down tightly to hide their eyes'. Victorian 'cures' included administering to young boys camphor, potassium bromide and the promotion of healthy eating habits and lots of fresh air.

Victorians were great inventors of gadgets and Professor Beckford Travis found fame in the medical world for his self-abuse alarm. An elaborate system of wires and a small box attached to a young man's penis allowed worried parents to hear a buzzer in their room if the member stirred during the night. History does not recall how commercially successful the system was.

Art Simon of Dallas, Texas, suffered one of the most painful castrations of recent times when his wife attacked him with a machete whilst he was in the shower at their home. As he fell to the floor his penis, hanging literally by a few threads, became firmly wedged in the drain and a surgeon had to separate the mashed member on the spot after emergency services failed to unplug it. Unlike most modern castration stories that end happily, his organ was way beyond repair and Simon remains a eunuch.

Codpieces, popular in the Middle Ages with men, were designed to give the impression of a permanent hard-on. Many were decorated with jewels and embroidery. Cod was an ancient word for scrotum.

Anthropologists claim that women use lipstick to redden their lips to create the image of their swollen labia when sexually aroused.

17
SPACE ALIENS

Howard Menger found fame in the US in the 1950s with his tales of contact with aliens. He claimed that as a child growing up in New England he had been visited by a beautiful blonde from outer space who arranged for other interstellar visitors to seek him out so he could provide them with earthling hairstyles, allowing them to mingle with the population. As a reward for his services he was given a trip to the moon which he said had an atmosphere which was quite breathable. He returned with a selection of lunar potatoes which it was claimed contained five times more protein than the terrestrial variety.

Residents of the US town of Fyffe, Alabama, claimed that in February 1989 the recently departed flamboyant pianist Liberace appeared in their town from the skies. The foppish ivory-tinkler was almost twelve feet in size and descended from a golden, banana-shaped spacecraft. A magical escalator conveyed him to earth level as he performed songs from the shows on a floating piano. News of the visitation spread like wildfire throughout the area and police were called to clear a jam of an estimated 4,000 cars along the roads into the town centre.

Mrs Cynthia Appleton of Birmingham, England, claimed that extra-terrestials visited her living room in 1957. A figure materialised in front of the fireplace wearing what

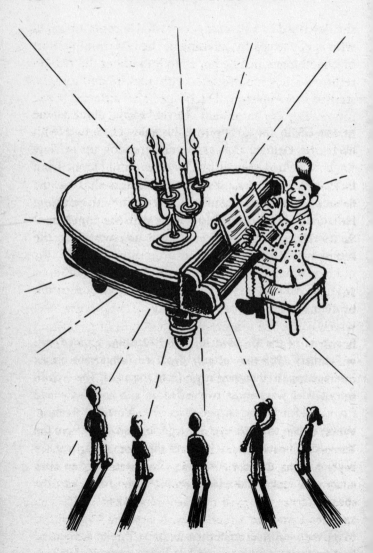

Liberace makes a comeback.

she described as a silver mackintosh. He communicated with her by telepathy, advising her he was running short of something which he hoped to find under the sea. He returned a few months later with a friend and told the startled Mrs Appleton of bloodshed and suffering in the future. He also informed her she would have a son Matthew who would spiritually belong to a race who live on Venus.

In 1968 the son of an Argentinian farmer working in the fields was confronted by space aliens with transparent legs. He was handed a note which he claimed was signed by F. Saucer. The stark message contained therein was, 'You shall know the world.'

John H. Womack of Alabama claimed he was abducted by aliens in 1975 and given a guided tour of their UFO which contained a formidable collection of giants and bearded dwarfs rescued from other planets. Womack was told a collection of human beings had been ruled out because they were thought to be too belligerent and selfish.

Whilst driving through Virginia, USA, lorry driver Harry Joe Turner claimed he was taken to a planet 2.5 light years beyond Alpha Centauri. He was interrogated by an alien entity who spoke 'like a tape recorder played backwards at speed'. Turner was given the alien name Alpha La 200 Lou and then treated to a tour of space including a special trip to the moon to view the footprints of the Apollo astronauts. Back on earth a medical examination showed that Turner was suffering from hysterical personality disorder.

'You shall know the world. F. Saucer.'

Brazilian farmer Antonio Villas Boas claims he was abducted by aliens in October 1957 for sexual purposes whilst out ploughing a field. A large red star descended on him and he was led struggling into a spacecraft by a marauding gang of five aliens. After being stripped and sponged down he was led to a room where a naked female lay on a bed. Boas claimed, 'She was more beautiful than any I have ever seen.' With alluring white hair and red underarm hair and pubes the galactic goddess took him in her arms but permitted no kissing. After biting him on the chin she pointed to her stomach and then the sky. He was given a lightning guided tour of the solar system before being returned to his field.

In October 1954 Mrs Jennie Roestenberg and her two children of Ranton, Shrewsbury, claimed a UFO buzzed their house. Mrs Roestenberg claimed she could see the occupants clearly. They were pale with shoulder length hair and wore what looked like ski suits with transparent helmets.

Farmer Gary T. Wilcox of Tioga City, New York, claimed he met aliens in 1964 whilst muckspreading. They had a long conversation on the subject of manure and fertiliser and advised him the soil on their planet was very rocky. Wilcox later left some fertiliser near their landing area which they later returned for to green up their planet.

Former US President Jimmy Carter claimed he saw a UFO in January 1969 whilst preparing to address a meeting in Leary, Georgia. He said, 'It was the darndest thing I've ever seen, it was big, it was very bright, it changed colours and it was about the size of the moon. We watched it for ten minutes but none of us could figure out what it was.'

Uri Geller and a Dr Andrija Puharich claim to have contacted aliens whilst Geller was put under a hypnotic spell by Puharich. During 1971 and 1972 he spoke to many cosmic beings and was told he would receive a cosmic brain. Plans for a massed landing on earth were also revealed, details of which would be passed on to the intrepid duo.

One of the earliest UFO sightings in the US took place at Galisto Junction, New Mexico, in 1880. The Santa Fe *Weekly New Mexican* reported the sighting of a strange object hovering near the ground. Onlookers heard the sounds of a party taking place on board and objects were tossed overboard that included silk embroidery and cups. A mysterious Chinese man appeared at the scene later and claimed the embroidery contained a message from his fiancé who was on board on a trip from China to New York.

At 5.12 p.m. on 26 November 1977 a voice from outer space interrupted the Southern Television early evening news. Gramaha, the representative of a mysterious planetary race, warned viewers in the ITV region not to listen to false prophets and guides and to beware of the planet passing into a new age of Aquarius. They were told, 'Listen to the voice of truth which is within you and you will lead yourselves on the path of evolution.' He signed off with, 'May you be blessed by the supreme love and truth of the cosmos.' The police could later find no trace of any interference with transmitters and TV technicians were baffled.

South African Elizabeth Klarer claimed that in the 1930s she had an affair with an alien heart-throb called Akon who literally swept her off her feet when his spacecraft landed on her farm. She was whisked away to live on the planet Meto and gave birth to a space son called Ayling. Returning to Earth she was often visited by her son and his space dad. Akon told her he was a midwife and that he rarely mated with earth women but did so to strengthen his race and infuse new blood.

Joe Simonton, a plumber of Eagle River, Wisconsin, claimed he saw a UFO hovering over his backyard in 1961. Three aliens appeared indicating they needed water. He noticed they were cooking pancakes and was given four of them before they took off. Scientific analysis showed they were made of flour, sugar and grease.

UFO sightings reached a peak in the US in 1951 when the sci-fi thriller film *The Day the Earth Stood Still* was released.

In 1950 *The Times* reported on a village in Basles, France which witnessed a display of flying saucers which left a luminous wake in the sky. Villagers claimed the extra-terrestrial display was linked by a coordinated backing of strange organ music.

Many UFO enthusiasts in the US are convinced that alien beings are involved in the highest levels of government. They claim that the EBEs (Extra-terrestrial biological entities) killed President Kennedy in 1963 as he was about to reveal all about them to the American public. President Eisenhower was alleged to have signed an initial treaty with them in the 1950s with their leader, His Omnipotent Highness Krull. The treaty ruled that EBES could abduct humans for biological testing but must always return them to Earth unharmed.

On 6 July 1874 townsfolk in Oxaca, Mexico claimed they saw a 400-foot trumpet hovering in the sky.

Anti-comet pills were sold in the US for a $1 a time to prevent the ill-effects expected from Halley's Comet.

18
UGLY

Research in Australia shows that pigs are delicate, sensitive animals who are often irritated by the actions of human beings towards them. Pig psychologist Graham Coleman has found pigs get angry having their rumps slapped, preferring friendly pats and strokes. Australian farmers have launched a pat-a-pig scheme to produce calmer porkers who supply fatter and tastier bacon.

Nineteenth-century Siamese twins Eng and Chang settled in England after a career on the US carnival circuit and married English wives. After being pursued by a nymphomaniac called Miss Gloria who published erotic poetry about them they fled to North Carolina where they set up separate homes on a farmstead. They each shared a bedroom for three in each house, Eng fathering twelve children, Chang ten. They grew to hate each other but were too old to be medically separated and they died in 1874 aged sixty-three.

Dr Preissman, a Victorian medical man, claimed in 1877 that a trained nose could pick up an odour on the breath up to six hours after a male or female had had intercourse. He claimed that this was due to a secretion from the buccal glands in the mouth. It was most common in men aged around thirty-five and could be smelt from a distance of four to six feet.

A hermaphrodite is a person with the sex organs of both the male and female. A popular carnival sideshow attraction was Billie Christina who boasted a flat male chest on his left side with a large female breast on his right. This image was cultivated with a left-sided crew cut and long tresses on the opposite side. He/she also shaved on just the Billie side.

Samuel D. Parks was billed as Hopp the Frog Boy because of his remarkable resemblance to a bullfrog.

Twenty-one-inch-tall General Tom Thumb once slept with Napoleon III's cockney mistress Cora Pearl. She had him delivered to her room on a silver serving platter.

Nineteenth-century adventurer Wilhelm Horn discovered a 'pig-girl' in 1831. The girl, in her early twenties, was discovered living in a hog-sty and had taken on the attributes of the animal, and grunted continually.

The shaving of underarm hair by women was a trend that began in the US. It has never been popular in Mediterranean countries where hair is seen to heighten the desire of males.

Siamese twins Lucio and Simplicio found fame by marrying twin sisters and performing a skating and tango act. One night one of them caused a carriage accident in which a child was run over. A judge, unable to decide which was the non-guilty brother, imposed a heavy fine causing the twins to take on

'Go on. Give us a kiss!'

a heavy work-load, much to the chagrin of the innocent brother. He threatened to give up work but had to concede defeat when the other threatened suicide.

The Medical Society of Oslo reported in 1895 on a woman of fifty-four who was found to have a tooth growing in her nose.

Many Victorian doctors specialising in VD claimed they could detect a person suffering from syphilis solely by the odour they emitted.

Grace McDaniels was known as the Mule-Faced Woman and was billed as the Ugliest Woman in the World. She was a popular feature of US carnivals and fairs. Her appearance was described thus by a journalist, 'Her flesh was like red raw meat, her huge chin was twisted at such a distorted angle she could hardly move her jaws. Her teeth were jagged and sharp and her nose was large and crooked. The objects which made her most look like a mule were her huge lips. Her eyes stared grotesquely in their deep-set sockets. All in all she was a sickening horrible sight.' Women and men often fainted when her veil was removed. Despite her looks she had a great personality and many who met her forgot her looks after a short time. She married a handsome man and had a son who managed her affairs. She died in 1958.

Prostitutes in nineteenth-century brothels in Paris, regularly shaved their pubic hair to decrease the chances of contracting disease. They regularly wore luxuriant and colourful pubic wigs which could be seen hanging from clothes lines on wash days.

Another person billed as 'The Ugliest Woman in the World' was Julia Pastrana. She fell in love with her manager who, reluctant to lose her, agreed to marry her. She died in childbirth but her manager/husband had both bodies stuffed to exhibit them throughout Europe.

In 1986 the Ugliest College Man Contest was held in Indiana, Pennsylvania. The first prize was $50 to be used for plastic surgery.

The Academies Des Sciences of Paris has the world's largest collection of toenails. Their prize exhibit is a left-footed big toe-nail which measures 4 ¾ inches.

Leonardo Da Vinci's portrait of the Mona Lisa is probably the most famous painting in the world and many theories have been put forward to explain the beauty of her enigmatic smile. Experts have claimed she was pregnant, suffering from Bell's palsy or was in the early stages of cholesterol poisoning. Art critics have also come up with the theory that Da Vinci was not very good at drawing lips and his painting went horribly wrong.

King Henry IV of France suffered from bromidrosis (an excess of sweat particularly from the feet). The smell was compared to that of rotting dead flesh. His second wife

A Nose for Winning – Student Hunch Pays Off.

Marie De Medici swathed their bedroom with flowers on their wedding night.

James Morris was known as the 'India Rubber Man' when he appeared as part of Barnum & Bailey's circus. He could pull skin from his chin, neck, nose, arms and legs almost eighteen inches away from his body.

Joannes and Lazarus Baptista were born in 1617 in Geneva. Both were baptised but Lazarus was a small appendage attached to the side of Joannes body.

Claude Seurat was displayed as 'The Living Skeleton'. He existed on a daily diet of a roll and a glass of wine. He measured just three inches from chest to spine, with his heartbeat clearly visible. His biceps measured just four inches.

Some diseases are said to emit their own distinctive smells. Typhus has an odour of honey; diabetes, apples; and dysentery, sweat and excrement.

Charles Tripp, 'The Armless Wonder', and Eli Bowen, 'The Legless Wonder', were a popular act in the nineteenth century, appearing immaculately suited riding a tandem bike with Tripp pedalling and Bowen steering.

The *British Medical Journal* of 1889 contained an article by a Dr Bechlinger who outlined the case of a 25-year-old woman from Martinique who had three legs and two vaginas.

In the nineteenth century Juan Baptista Dos Santos was born with two oversized penises and a third leg. He had an intense sex life, after climaxing with one penis he continued with his second model.

It was believed that over-sexed males who suffered from satyriasis secreted semen through their sweat glands.

Jo-Jo the Dog Faced Boy was a major carnival attraction in the US. Compared in appearance to a Skye Terrier his face was covered in silky yellow hair.

Rosa and Josepha Blazek were Siamese twins who shared one anal orifice but each had a vagina. One could sleep whilst the other remained awake. Unbeknown to her sister Rosa had sex with a Viennese butcher and had a child by him. All four made a special appearance at the Theatre De La Gaite in Paris to sell-out audiences.

Gynaecomastia is the enlargement of male breasts to female proportions. It is common that as these breasts increase in size the genitals begin to shrink.

Sufferers from microcephalus, a disease that caused a receding forehead and a small skull were exhibited in the US as 'pinheads'. One of the most famous was Zip whose cone shaped head was topped off with a Red Indian styled topknot. His career lasted sixty-seven years until his death in 1926. Many pinheads appeared in Tod Browning's infamous horror film *Freaks* in 1932. They included Maggie, Last of the Aztecs, Elvira and Jenny Lee Snow and Pipo and Zipo.

A popular 1890s sideshow exhibit was a twenty-year-old Indian boy called Laloo. He suffered from parasitic terata where a normal human being has part of a second body issuing from the stomach region. Laloo's growth consisted of a group of intestines, an anus and a well developed penis which passed water and became erect unbeknown to its owner.

Victorian doctors often debated whether it was possible to suffer a fracture of the penis. A Dr Keen and a Dr White claimed the male urethra could be ruptured during violent intercourse particularly if a woman positioned herself on top of the man.

A common injury in Victorian times was for manhood to be lost from the kick of a horse's hoof. Predominantly the accident occurred to military men, particularly in artillery regiments.

George II is famed as being the only British monarch to die on the lavatory after he collapsed and hit his head on a board in 1760. His loyal German valet who stood outside the lavatory each time the ruler took to his other throne told court officials he had heard a noise 'louder than the Royal wind' and guessed something was wrong.

In ancient Babylon fathers sold off their attractive

offspring at auction to potential husbands and used the money to give their uglier sisters dowries.

King Phillip the Fair of France passed a law that lepers or anyone suffering from skin disease should be executed.

A typical countryside cure in England for blackheads is to locate a bramble bush which forms an arch and on a sunny day crawl backwards and forwards under it three times east to west.

Scientists now believe that termites with flatulence are one of the major factors in the growth of global warming. They release through their insect bottoms almost a fifth of the world's production of methane gas, guaranteed to make anyone coming within a few yards of it pinch their nose and run. The pungent stench is a product of the average termite's diet which ranges from animal dung, rotting wood and dry grass to decaying leaves. Dr Paul Eggleton of London's Natural History Museum regularly makes trips to Africa to capture the termite's prolific output of wind. He transports his jars of termite farts through customs using the label 'Forest Air'.

Stella Walsh won Gold for Poland in the 1932 Olympic 100-metre race. She won numerous top track events over the next few years and finally settled in the US. She was found dead in a Cleveland parking lot in 1980 and at the post mortem the coroner discovered that the former athletic star had a full set of male genitals. The wedding tackle was so small however she/he had managed to pass as a female throughout less than rigorous medical tests in the 1930s. Sex testing is now compulsory at all major athletic events.

In the Middle Ages Japanese women used to paint their teeth black in order to attract men.

19
WALLIES

Affluent residents of Fleet, Hampshire, were inundated with piles of porn through their letterboxes after their postman Alan Fenney added the envelopes of filth to their daily deliveries of electricity bills and *Reader's Digest* prize draws. Fenney claimed he had been hired by a mysterious left-wing organisation to undermine the establishment. One recipient, Major General John Irving, said, 'I'd never seen anything like it since 1931 when a boy in the streets of Port Said showed me indecent pictures.'

The eight-man James-Younger gang were the scourge of the Wild West with a fifteen-year track record of successful heists. Their big mistake, however, was to rob the First National Bank of Northfield, Minnesota, in 1876. The irate inhabitants stood firm against the outlaws, shooting two dead and injuring five others. The gang broke up and were never a major force again.

Arthur Mandelko, aged twenty-four, was found dead in the fridge of his Hollywood home in 1970. He had become famous in his neighbourhood for his practice of dressing up as Superman at night and leaping across the roofs of houses. He also regularly donned a police uniform to patrol the streets on his pushbike, which was fitted out with a flashing blue light and siren. Police found a man-sized robot in his

Supersilly, Arthur Mandelko, came to a frozen end.

living room made of cardboard, rags and tape and also a vast collection of non-functioning electronic devices. His nearest neighbours had continually complained of incessant thumping noises emanating from his house throughout the night.

Langley and Homer Collyer were wealthy eccentrics who threw nothing out of their New York home. Langley cared for Homer who became a hopeless invalid in between constructing bizarre booby traps to satisfy his paranoia that their house was about to be invaded by intruders. Police later found the pair dead, Homer of malnutrition and Langley crushed to death underneath a sewing machine and weighted suitcases.

In San Jose, California, a family recently had their home cleaned by sanitation inspectors after they had collected over twenty-five tons of rubbish. Not content with having their own garbage the family of five visited local tips to increase their collection and also neighbours' bins. They even rented storage units to cope with the overflow. They expressed relief after the clean up so they could start again.

When Da Vinci's painting of the Mona Lisa was stolen from the Louvre in Paris in 1911 more people turned up over the next two years to look at the blank space on the wall than had come to see the picture previously.

In 1981 stage dwarf Barry Gnome, aged seventy-four, came out of retirement to play Dozy in a production

Dozing Dozy.

of *Snow White and the Seven Dwarfs*. At his comeback performance he was found to be asleep on stage and was taken to hospital to recover.

Pensioner Alec Parrott was voted Pub Bore of the Year in 1994 after being nominated by regulars at the White Hart Hotel in Hayle, Cornwall in answer to a competition in a brewing magazine. Mr Parrott achieved the honour because of his regular subjects of conversation: bus routes, timetables and his service in the army.

Model train fan John Whelan's marriage ended on his wedding night in Christchurch, New Zealand, when he refused to make love to his new wife, preferring instead to try out a new track layout for his train set.

General George Custer and the Seventh Cavalry were wiped out at the Battle of Little Big Horn in 1876 by Cheyenne and Sioux warriors. He told his men on sighting the Red Indian encampment, 'Hurrah boys, we've got them.' He had also stated in 1870, 'The army is the Indian's best friend.'

In the 1930s America gangster John Dillinger was named 'Public Enemy Number One' by the FBI. During five years on the run he robbed more banks than western outlaw Jesse James did in sixteen years. In 1934 along with Baby Face Nelson and others he raided the First National Bank in Mason City, Iowa. An alert cashier handed over the cash in low denomination notes and coins ensuring the robbers escaped with just $50,000 from a potential $250,000 haul. This fiasco ensured the gang laid low for some time until Dillinger was shot dead after being betrayed to the FBI some months later.

Bobbye D. Sorrells is the author of *The Nonsexist Communicator: Solving the Problems of Gender and Awkwardness in the English Language*. The book suggests the following alternatives for the word manslaughter – humanslaughter, personslaughter, wo/manslaughter or manslaughter and womanslaughter.

In 1976 the Arts Council gave three students £400 to walk around East Anglia with ten-foot yellow poles tied to their heads. One student told the press, 'We are not conning people just to get the money. If we had not got the grant we would probably have saved up the money and done it ourselves. It's an attempt to tread new ground in the art world.'

In 1977 President Idi Amin of Uganda mistook former Tory Prime Minister Ted Heath for his namesake, the 1950s band leader of the same name. A keen swing fan, Amin wanted the politician to come to Uganda to celebrate the anniversary of his military coup. A telegram stated that he understood he had been 'demoted to the obscure rank of music bandmaster' but he claimed, 'Mr Heath is one of the best bandmasters in Britain.' Payment was confirmed to be with goats, chickens and agricultural produce.

God delivered the Ten Commandments in less than 300 words, the American Declaration of Independence clocks in at about the same number. However, the EEC

Ordinance on the Importation of Caramel Sweets run to almost 25,911.

When President Bokassa, the ruler of the Central African Republic underwent his coronation in 1977 his gold throne alone was worth $30 million. The average income for his subjects was $250 a year.

When David and Brenda Powell thought they heard the sound of a cat trapped behind a wall of their three-bedroomed house they called in International Rescue, an organisation who usually operate at earthquakes and natural disasters. Armed with thermal imaging equipment and mini cameras they knocked holes in the walls throughout the house and lifted floorboards to no avail. After virtually destroying the property they assumed the cat had escaped by a secret exit or had died of shock at the sounds of destruction.

At the time of writing the Cones Hotline introduced by John Major and the Department of Transport to great fanfare has so far only resulted in three sets of cones being removed. Motorists were encouraged to ring the hotline if they spotted cones being used unnecessarily but fewer than thirty calls a day are made. A caller complaining about an abundance of cones on the A21 in Kent rang the number twenty-nine times before someone answered their call. They were told the cones were there 'probably because of road works'.

US senator Howell Heflin made a major political error at a recent press conference. Sweating profusely under television lighting he reached into the front pocket of his jacket for a handkerchief and produced a pair of female knickers. The quick thinking senator claimed that they belonged to his wife, a remark that was met by howels of derision from the press corps.

British Rail recently came up with one of their best excuses ever for the late arrival of a train. The passengers on the 19.10 service from Cardiff to Birmingham could hardly believe their ears when they were told that their train, already forty minutes late, was stopping seven miles short of Birmingham because the driver had lost his way. British Rail later confirmed that the driver had been diverted on to a stretch of track he was unfamiliar with and because he did not have 'route knowledge' had to be substituted by a relief driver.

In 1973 artist Carl Andre exhibited his work 'American Decay' at a US art gallery. It consisted of 500 lbs of cottage cheese, ten inches deep, on a piece of tar paper and covered in ten gallons of ketchup. The exhibition lasted only one day after the gallery was evacuated because of the smell.

Four people died in 1974 in Uttar Pradesh, India, when they travelled to a wedding party on the back of an elephant. In high spirits they cracked open a bottle of champagne and also gave some to the elephant through its trunk. The crazed pachyderm began to stagger and then ran into a high tension power cable, electrocuting the passengers.

Mathematician William Shanks spent fifteen years of

his life completing the calculation of the value of pi to 707 decimal places. Later research showed that his last 100 digits were incorrect.

A fifteen-year-old teenager could not believe his luck when he appeared in front of magistrates in Mold, North Wales, on charges of kicking and headbutting a smaller boy. Instead of a custodial sentence he was sent on a martial arts course, all part of a package of pioneering 'temper control' courses planned by social workers at Clwyd County Council. The bench also recommended that the youth attend 'mediation sessions' with his victim so he could sort out his aggressive behaviour.

Two OAPs fought a duel in Cleveland, Ohio in 1981 in the hallway of their apartment block using antique pistols. Standing five feet apart they blasted away at each other firing six bullets each but missed each other completely. One was partially blind and the other supported himself on a stick.

A British Parliamentary Committee set up in 1878 to review Thomas Edison's invention the light bulb concluded, 'It is good enough for our transatlantic friends but unworthy of the attention of practical or scientific men.'

Eighteen-year-old Ian Ord thought he might escape with just a fine from Teesside Crown Court when he appeared on a charge of car theft. However he was remanded in custody for a retrial because he could not stop laughing every time someone spoke while his case was heard. His lawyer apologised for his client's behaviour claiming he suffered from a 'nervous disorder'.

Ron Arnold of Faversham, Kent, ended up red faced when he applied for a job as a steward on 'Le Shuttle', the Channel Tunnel express train linking Britain and France. The application form requested a full length photograph of each applicant but Ron became totally confused and sent in a naked full-frontal pose. Surprised officials were sympathetic over the display of his appendages but he didn't get the job.

Former US Vice President Dan Quayle was once asked if he had considered becoming a Jehovah's Witness. He replied to his questioner that he couldn't help because he didn't see the accident.

American Tom Dumont bought Trafalgar Square in 1923 from con man Arthur Ferguson for £6,000. He was given the whole site as a job lot including Nelson's-column, the lions and the fountains because as Scotsman Ferguson told him, Britain had to reduce the National Debt. Ferguson later succeeded in selling Big Ben, the Statue of Liberty and a lease on the White House.

French artist Christian Boltanski held an unusual art exhibition at London's Serpentine Gallery called Take Me (I'm Yours). It consisted of two tons of secondhand clothes assembled in piles by the artist, 35,000 photocopied pictures and a selection of fruit. Members of the public were invited to spend £1 on a carrier bag and help themselves to as much of the exhibits as they wanted. Gallery boss Hans Obrist said, 'It's meant to be a process of continual transformation. Some people will come in and perceive the gallery as a secondhand clothes shop, others will see the piles of clothes as art.' The exhibition's catalogue claimed the show focused on 'the dual code of the iconographic and the functional aspect of art, wherby the homogeneity of the work of art is compromised by the heterogeneity of its potential uses'.

The Society for Indecency to Naked Animals was formed in the US in the 1950s mainly as a joke but it later attracted members who took to demonstrating for their cause. In 1963 they marched outside the White House in order to make President Kennedy order that clothing should be placed on horses appearing in public. In 1992 the town of Saint Augustine in Florida passed a law which required all horses that pulled tourist carriages through the town to wear nappies.

Thomas Flaherty, an Irish labourer, escaped a prison sentence at St Albans Crown Court after the judge was told he had stolen a consignment of microwave ovens in the mistaken belief they were television sets. The judge ordered his release as he felt it was unfair to let someone so simple go to prison.

In 1976 23,000 people were killed when a huge earthquake rocked Guatemala. The UN and various US relief agencies delivered a consignment of 115 tons of medical supplies to the stricken Guatamelan authorities who became very confused on opening the variety of boxes. The bulk of the aid consisted of pills manufactured in 1934 with no indication as to what ailments they cured, drug sampler packs previously sent to American doctors and a large selection of condoms. Three pharmacists spent over three months trying to make sense of the wide range of pharmaceutical items but in the end gave up and employed bulldozers to consign everything to a hole in the ground.

Tracy Craig, aged thirty, of Carlisle received three years in prison for stealing £830 from the Cumberland Building Society. The police said that she had been easily caught because her holdup outfit made her resemble Noddy and her getaway had been witnessed by many passers-by.

The Brazilian Treasury stopped issuing one cruzeiro bank notes in 1960 when it was discovered that it cost 1.2 cruzeiros to print each one.

Musical conductor Jean Baptiste Lully was famed for beating out the rhythm of classical pieces with a pointed cane when rehearsing orchestras. One day he misjudged a beat, pinned his foot to the floor and died of blood poisoning.

20
WACKY
ORGANISATIONS

After a hard day's work in the studio there's nothing I like more than getting out my tweezers and magnifying glass and rearranging my stamp albums. My particular interest is in prewar first day covers of Trinidad and Tobago and also used second-class British stamps from 1978.

You'll be amazed in this section with what other people do in their spare time.

The Barbed Wire Collector magazine is published in Texas every month. Each company manufacturing barbed wire throughout the world makes each type to its own unique design and wire enthusiasts avidly wait for new types of wire to come on the market. The magazine has a section called Fence Facts and married couples are invited to send in a photo of themselves for the 'Prickly Pair of the Month' feature.

The International Brick Collectors Association in Columbia, Missouri, has members across the world. Founder Henry Holt boasts a collection of over 5,000 different bricks.

Fans of Richard III meet in Haywards Heath to discuss their favourite British monarch. They publish a magazine called *The Rickardian*.

The Bruce Forsyth Social Club is based in Plymouth and has

Barbed passion.

over fifty members. It was founded by banker Mike Colwill, and the official greeting used by all members is, 'Nice to see you, to see you nice.' The club meets every two months to play their own version of *The Generation Game* wearing pieces of carpet on their heads. When Brucie himself visited Plymouth in 1990 to play golf he met a selection of members but thought he had been set up by comic colleague Ronnie Corbett.

The Sausage Appreciation Society based in London will travel the length and breadth of Great Britain in their search for the perfect banger. Barbara Windsor is an honorary member and their club magazine tackles such subjects as 'To Prick or Not To Prick' and includes a section on songs which celebrate the sausage.

Simon Cole and John Kavyo founded The Crossroads Appreciation Society in Bournemouth. Members meet under the watchful gaze of an oil painting of Amy Turtle and the original motel sign (Crossroads Motel – Bar Restaurant and Swimming Pool – Open To Non-Residents) graces their front door. Each year they make a pilgrimage to Noele Gordon's grave. The society were keen to buy the original Crossroads Motel register but changed their minds when they discovered it was just full of doodles.

The Decimal Time Society was founded in Hampshire by Mike Pinder. All members are sworn to canvass for a ten-hour day, a hundred-minute hour and a ten-day week.

The Street Lamp Interference Exchange compiles a dossier on

people who have the power to switch off streetlights merely by walking past them. Founder Hilary Evans, a paranormal researcher, has yet to meet anyone who has achieved or witnessed this strange feat.

The Eurovision Song Contest fan club has over 500 members who often spend time listening to such entries as Finland's 'Don't Drop the Bomb On Me' or Yugoslavia's 'Come On and Put On Your Levis'. A particular favourite is the Greek entry whose subject matter was about a Turkish napalm attack in Cyprus.

The Test Card Circle in Edinburgh has over 100 members who are devoted to the study and appreciation of television test cards and music. They swap videos of their favourite cards and enjoy listening to the obscure library music which accompanies them. A highlight of their year is Test Card Mastermind where competitors are quizzed on such subjects as which type of aerials are most likely to cause ghosting. Answer buzzers are set to reproduce tone frequencies for BBC transmitters.

The Glossopoeic Quarterly is a magazine published in Minnesota which is devoted to fictional languages. Members spend their time speaking verbal inventions such as Valrast, a mixture of Spanish and Latin, or Bzhaghitakh, six levels of two-tone words mixing guttural Arabic and tonal Chinese.

The George Formby Society meet regularly to have ukulele

'Honest Guv, I never touched it!'

sessions indulging in joint strumming sessions on such greats as 'With My Little Stick of Blackpool Rock', 'Leaning on a Lamp Post' and 'Mother What'll I Do Now?' Ex-Beatle George Harrison is a member and often joins in on their 'Turned Out Nice Again' sessions.

The Janet Ellis fanzine is published in Poole and is devoted to the life and works of the popular ex-Blue Peter presenter. Founder Nicholas Hall fell for her when she appeared in a 1978 episode of TV cop series *The Sweeney*. Features in the magazine include a Janet crossword, articles on her asthma problem and a top ten of the favourite outfits she has worn.

Jonathan King, famed for his naff pop hits such as 'Johnny Reggae', 'Leap Up and Down and Wave Your Knickers in the Air' and 'Loop Di Love' has his very own fan club in Rochdale.

The Pillar-Box Study Group meet regularly in Birmingham to talk of the latest news in the pillar-box world and exchange photographs of pillar-boxes across the UK and the world. Founder member Ron Hall is famed for his survey of pillar-boxes in Leamington Spa.

The Maledicta Society in Santa Rosa, California, conduct academic studies of abusive language. Subjects they tackle include Talking Dirty in Cuban Spanish, Greek Fist-Phallus Gestures, and Swearing in Australian Football. They are currently working on a glossary of farting euphemisims.

Members of the Narrow Bandwith Television Association in Derbyshire enjoy nothing more than promoting the development, study and use of low definition TVs that were first seen in the 1920s and 1930s. They're not interested in Sony Trinitrons or Fastext. They're happier searching for better quality 32-line pictures. They meet at an annual convention where they transmit and receive images on their antique machines. The Association is truly an international brotherhood with a large contingent of Dutch members.

The Polite Society in Staffordshire enjoy meeting and being polite to each other. Their club badge depicts a man doffing his hat.

Pun Intended Quarterly based in Texas has over 2,000 members who meet each year for the American Pun-Making Championships. They sit around in groups, chose a subject and pun away for the rest of the day.

Members of the National Fancy Rat Society in Croydon are fans of rats large and small. They compete for the Fanciest Rat title, produce rat-themed Christmas cards and offer health hints for owners of sickly rats.

The Dental History Society is based in Wimpole Street, London, and publishes a monthly magazine for its members. Articles include such topics as 'Dentists in seventeenth-century Holland', '150 Years of Anaesthesia' and 'The History of Dentistry in Western Painting'. Their museum includes one of the world's finest collections of false teeth and a section on eighteenth-century dentist Martin Van Butchell who kept the embalmed body of his wife in his waiting room.